FELICIA CARTRIGHT

AND THE
TROUBLED RANCHER

Felicia   Joan

FELICIA CARTRIGHT

AND THE
TROUBLED RANCHER

BERNARD PALMER

ANEKO
PRESS

Cover Artwork: Adobe Firefly & Ideogram
Editor: Charlene Miskimen

Aneko Press Youth

www.anekopress.com

Aneko Press, Life Sentence Publishing, and our logos are trademarks of
Life Sentence Publishing, Inc.
203 E. Birch Street
P.O. Box 652
Abbotsford, WI 54405

JUVENILE FICTION / Religious / Christian / Action & Adventure

Paperback ISBN: 979-8-88936-300-2
eBook ISBN: 979-8-88936-301-9

10   9   8   7   6   5   4   3   2   1

Available where books are sold

CONTENTS

CHAPTER 1

VACATION DREAMS

Felicia Cartright turned quite deliberately from the dormitory window, her back toward the campus of the Wellington School for Girls. Her young face clouded.

"What did Miss Duncan say, Joan?"

Her roommate, Joan Bailey, shrugged her shoulders and crossed to the desk.

"You know how Miss Duncan is, Felicia. Edna met me in the hall and said that Miss Duncan had sent her to find you and me and ask us to come to her office at our earliest convenience."

"Not much help, is it?"

Felicia surveyed her image in the mirror, tucked an imaginary strand of hair into place, and fumbled with the catch on the necklace her mother had sent for her birthday.

"I knew that biology exam was a stinger," she murmured, "but I was almost positive I had passed it."

"Look who's worrying about grades," Joan scoffed. "If that has you talking to yourself, I'd just as well pack up and get ready to go home."

"Summer vacation starts in a week, and you've already got your things packed. Remember?"

"You know what I meant."

A deep sigh escaped her lips.

"Oh, well, these years at Wellington have been the best years of my life." Joan pouted a little. "When I'm old and gray and crippled with arthritis, I'll think back to this day when my heart was broken, never to be healed again."

"Why else would she call us down to her office," Felicia asked, "and insist that we come as soon as possible?"

"Maybe she's lonesome for us," Joan answered. "She's probably come to the place where she can't live another hour without seeing our angelic faces."

"Can't you be sensible just for once?"

Joan got to her feet.

"I know just how Daniel felt when they dumped him into the lions' den."

They left their room and went down to the main floor to Miss Duncan's office. The outside door of the old building was open. The girls stopped at the foot of the stairs and looked out on the bright new green of spring.

"Listen to those birds," Felicia said. "Isn't this a beautiful day?"

"Too beautiful for an execution," Joan muttered.

Felicia's pulse quickened perceptibly as she opened the door, and they stepped into the office of the dean of women.

"Maybe she's not in," Joan whispered hopefully.

But Miss Duncan was in her private office. The inner door was ajar, revealing her at her desk, studying a letter intently. It was a moment or two before she realized anyone was waiting to see her. The scowl on her face deepened as she read, and she went back over portions a second time. It was then that her eye caught a glimpse of them, and she smiled disarmingly.

"I'm sorry to have kept you waiting," she said with just the right note of regret in her voice.

"That's quite all right."

"Won't you sit down?" She indicated chairs and waited until the girls were seated. Then she leaned forward, resting her elbows on the desk and clasping her hands in a characteristic pose.

"I suppose you are wondering why I called you in so near the close of the school term," she began.

"To tell you the truth," Joan replied nervously, "I was afraid my past was finally catching up with me. I thought you were about to inform me that for the good of Wellington School for Girls, I was receiving a formal request to make myself obnoxious at another school next year."

The smile came once more to Miss Duncan's face.

"You may rest easily until fall, at least, Miss Bailey," she said. "We noted a small but definite improvement in your grades. Not enough to make us or you satisfied, mind you. But there was a bit of encouragement."

Joan expelled her breath slowly.

"That's a relief."

"I have quite a different matter to talk with you girls about," Miss Duncan went on. She picked up the envelope from her desk and removed the letter.

"I wanted to talk with you about a letter I received this morning from a woman who was an old schoolmate of mine here at Wellington, Abigail Chandler. Her name was Johnson when I knew her here at school."

Felicia and Joan looked at one another inquisitively.

"Abigail and her husband had a ranch out in Colorado," Miss Duncan continued. "I believe they called it a working ranch, a ranch that runs cattle. In addition, they were set up as a small dude ranch. They built a main lodge and a few modern cabins so they could take in paying guests."

She hesitated, studying first Felicia and then Joan.

"That's very interesting," Joan said frankly, "but just exactly how does this concern us?"

"Don't be so impatient, Miss Bailey. I'm coming to that."

Miss Duncan picked up the letter once more and scanned its contents.

"Abigail's husband died last winter after a long illness," she continued.

"Oh, that's too bad," Felicia said.

"A real tragedy," Miss Duncan said softly. "He was an outstanding Christian."

She returned the letter to the envelope before continuing.

"Things haven't been too easy for Abigail," Miss Duncan went on at last. "They have had a protracted drought the past three years and have had to sell off all the cattle except the foundation herd. She has had an offer to buy the ranch, but has decided to keep it and increase the number of paying guests until the drought is over."

"And how do we figure in that?" Felicia asked.

"Abigail wrote asking me to select two Wellington young ladies who would like to help her as hostesses at the Lazy Bar Y. I thought of you girls immediately – that is, if you are free for the summer."

Felicia's eyes widened.

"Do–do you really mean that?" Joan asked. "You aren't joking?"

Miss Duncan's face grew stern.

"Miss Bailey, I allow myself a bit of levity with the girls now and then, but I can assure you that I do not joke with them in such a manner."

Her features relaxed a little.

"It won't be necessary for you to give me an answer tonight. You may talk it over and consider it until nine thirty tomorrow morning. That will give me ample time to answer."

Felicia's eyes met Joan's.

"I don't think we have to wait to give you an answer, Miss Duncan," Felicia said. "If it's all right with Joan, I know I can make it."

Joan smiled wistfully.

"I always did wonder if those cowboys were as handsome as people say they are."

"Knowing you, Miss Bailey," the dean of women said curtly, "I shall pretend you did not make that remark. It is unbecoming to a well-bred Wellington Girl."

She glanced down at the letter once more.

"If you wish that to be your answer, I shall write Abigail tonight. If not, I shall be very glad to wait until the morning."

* * *

There was a flurry of activity during the next few days as Felicia and Joan made ready for the trip to Denver.

"I wish we could drive out," Joan said, looking at her red convertible.

"We'll be riding horseback," Felicia reminded her.

At last the day for their departure arrived, and Miss Duncan drove them to the airport.

"I've always wanted to go to a dude ranch," Joan said, her voice taut with excitement.

"So have I," Felicia replied. "And the nice thing is that we won't be paying for our stay there. Instead, we'll actually be earning money."

Joan giggled.

"When I called Dad and told him about it, he said he was sure there must be some mistake. I think he had his doubts that anyone would want to hire me to work for them."

The plane ride from Boston to Denver was uneventful. Almost as soon as they got into the air, it seemed to Felicia and Joan that the big jet was nosing down to land at the Denver airport.

"Now, if Mrs. Chandler is only here to meet us," Felicia said, glancing out the window.

"There she is," Joan put in, pointing out a gray-haired woman about Miss Duncan's age who was standing alone at the gate.

Felicia studied the woman for a brief minute.

"How do you know?" she asked.

"I can recognize her by the Wellington look." Joan smiled at Felicia. "Haven't you observed the crisp, correct, self-confident appearance of a Wellington graduate? Miss Duncan would be ashamed of you."

The plane came to a stop, and the passengers began to gather their belongings.

"We'll soon see whether you pass or flunk," Felicia whispered.

They left the plane and walked to the gate. Sure enough, the gray-haired woman approached and intercepted them.

"I take it that you are Miss Cartright and Miss Bailey," she said crisply.

"That's right," Felicia answered. "I'm Felicia, and this is Joan. Then you are Mrs. Chandler."

The woman smiled briefly.

"I'm Mrs. Chandler," she admitted, "but everyone calls me Aunt Abigail."

They walked over to the counter to claim the girls' luggage.

"We're so glad you wanted someone from Wellington," Felicia said, "and that Miss Duncan gave us the opportunity to come."

A troubled look deepened the lines in Aunt Abigail's sallow face. And for an instant, the fire in her eyes died away.

"From the way things have been going," she said, "I'm not sure there'll be much work to do. You may be the only guests we have at the ranch by the time we get back there."

She laughed again, but it was a hollow, empty laugh.

CHAPTER 2

THE DISGRUNTLED GUEST

While they were waiting for their luggage, Felicia had tried to study Mrs. Chandler. She was half a head taller than Miss Duncan, but struck from the same mold. Hers was a powerful body, lean and sparsely built.

She had a calm, serene confidence about her, and she gave the appearance of being as accustomed to helping brand calves or rope mavericks as she would be to preside over a luncheon or a formal dinner. Her hands were rough and reddened with work, and her hair was liberally streaked with gray. There was the look of bone weariness about her eyes, but the fire of courage gleamed there. She was one who could have trouble, but could say with John Paul Jones, "I have just begun to fight."

The luggage was brought in. The girls claimed theirs and carried it to the old truck in the parking lot.

"It's not much," Aunt Abigail observed brightly, "but it got me here, and it'll get us back."

They climbed into the seat beside her.

"I wish we could go straight back to the ranch," she said, "but we've got to meet the train."

"Do you have other workers coming?" Felicia asked.

"Not workers. Guests. I usually don't come all the way to Denver to pick up guests, but since I had to come in to get you girls, I told these girls that I'd pick them up too."

She sighed deeply.

"At least if I bring them out, we'll have someone there when we get back."

"That's the second time you've mentioned something like that," Felicia said, concern in her voice.

"Don't mind what I say," the woman answered. "We'll manage somehow."

She changed the subject quickly, but Felicia could not forget the tiredness in her face and the sag of her shoulders when she was not consciously straightening them.

The train came in shortly, and Aunt Abigail unerringly sorted out her guests and introduced herself and the girls to them.

"Here are Sherry Fowler and Rosetta Bloom."

Felicia and Joan acknowledged the introductions.

"I don't know what possessed Dad to send me out to this place," Rosetta said with a toss of her blond hair as they walked to the truck. I tried to talk him out of it, but it was no use. He told me I was coming, and that was that."

She shrugged her shoulders expressively.

"So, here I am."

Aunt Abigail ignored the displeasure in Rosetta's voice.

"We try to have good times at the Lazy Bar Y. I hope you will enjoy yourself with us."

Rosetta's cheeks dimpled condescendingly as she chose to flash a smile at the ranch woman.

"I'm certainly going to try," she said, "but really, what do you do to enjoy yourself in Outer Siberia?"

Felicia and Joan glanced at her disapprovingly.

"You can help in the salt mines," Aunt Abigail replied.

Felicia almost choked with laughter.

Their luggage safely stowed in the truck, they all got inside – Felicia in front with Mrs. Chandler and the three other girls in the back seat.

"Tell me," Rosetta began once more, "are there any cute cowboys at the ranch?"

"I'm sure their wives think so," Aunt Abigail said.

The girl frowned.

"I'm crushed already."

Joan turned in the seat to look at the girl.

"But then it will be a relief not to have boys underfoot all the time. Honestly, when I'm home, the phone's ringing every half hour or so. Dad's threatened to take it away."

Joan caught Sherry Fowler's eyes and winked. A faint smile was on the girl's face.

For a time, Rosetta settled back in the seat and lapsed into silence.

The other girls talked cheerfully.

When they were finally out of Denver on the highway headed west, Rosetta spoke again.

"Tell me," she said, keeping her voice low, "just what is there to do for excitement out at the Lazy Bar Y?"

"That's something we don't know for sure yet," Felicia explained, "but Aunt Abigail is so full of life I know there'll always be something to do."

"She told us they have horseback riding, swimming, climbing, exploring, camping trips, and that sort of thing," Joan put in. "It sounds as though there's something doing every minute."

A sneer made Rosetta's attractive young face seem almost ugly.

"That sounds positively devastating."

"It sounds like a lot of fun to me," Sherry put in.

"And to me," Joan said. "I can hardly wait."

"You probably would feel that way about it," Rosetta told them, "but I'm used to some *real* fun."

The ride out to the Lazy Bar Y was a long one, but the scenery was so beautiful the time passed quickly. The wide highway wound its way into the mountains some fifty or sixty miles. Just outside a little town, Aunt Abigail slowed, made a sharp right turn on a narrow, twisting gravel road, and headed up the ridge.

Rosetta glanced around uneasily.

"Are you sure this is the right road?"

Aunt Abigail chuckled.

"I've lived up here for over twenty years, my dear," she said gently.

"It's beautiful!" Sherry exclaimed.

Felicia and Joan nodded their agreement. Something about those majestic hills took the words from their lips.

They crossed the ridge and headed down into the valley on the other side.

"Doesn't this make you marvel at the wonders and the power of God?" Joan asked, a hush in her voice.

Rosetta surveyed her critically.

"Don't be medieval, Joan."

At the Lazy Bar Y, the girls separated and were shown to their rooms.

"Well," Joan said as soon as the door behind them was closed, "what do you think?"

"The place is beautiful."

"There aren't very many guests around, are there?"

"I can't understand why either. It's such a beautiful place."

They went to the window and looked out at the towering snow-shrouded peaks. They were still standing there when there was a light rap at the door, and Aunt Abigail came in.

She managed to smile, but it was a feeble, transparent effort that let the gloom show through. The girls both noticed it.

"Won't you sit down?" Joan suggested.

"No, thank you. I've only got a minute."

"Is there something we can do to help you?" Felicia asked.

"As a matter of fact, yes." She moved over to a chair and sat down. "You've met Rosetta Bloom."

The girls glanced at one another.

"Yes," Joan said, "we've met her."

Aunt Abigail's hands were nervously fidgeting with the hem of her shirt.

"I know she's not the most pleasant individual, but it's important that she have a good time here. It's very important."

It seemed to Felicia that the ranch woman's eyes clouded.

"You see," Aunt Abigail explained, "her father is the president of a large manufacturing company in Chicago. He's planning to come out for a short visit in two or three weeks. In his message, he indicated that he is considering the Lazy Bar Y as a place for his firm to send their top salesmen for vacations."

She paused, and it was a moment or two before she spoke again.

"If they do that, it will mean a great deal of business for us. Perhaps even enough to–to make the difference."

"I see," Felicia answered, only half understanding what she meant.

"So I'd really appreciate it if you girls would make a special effort to be nice to Rosetta and help her to enjoy herself."

"We'll do everything we can," Felicia assured her. "We've already made arrangements to have dinner with her and the Fowler girl this evening."

"Splendid," Aunt Abigail said, "and thank you."

Felicia and Joan dressed early for dinner and walked slowly to the lodge. Neither Sherry nor Rosetta was there, so they went in and sat at a table near the big picture window.

"You know," Joan said, "Aunt Abigail handed us a hot one. It's going to take some doing to show Rosetta a good time."

"But we've got to do what we can," Felicia replied.

Sherry came in soon, an attractive, dark-haired little elf with a manner as cheerful as her smile.

"I knocked on Rosetta's door," she said, pulling out a chair and seating herself at the table, "but she wasn't there. I thought she was already here."

"She'll be along in a few minutes," Felicia answered.

It wasn't long until the door opened and Rosetta came bouncing in angrily.

"And what's the matter with you?" Joan asked. "You look as though you've just tangled with a rabid coyote or a rattlesnake."

Jerking out a chair, Rosetta flounced into it.

"I'm so mad I–I–" she struggled for words. "I'm so mad I could spit!"

"Now what has brought all that on?"

She leaned forward.

"Do you know what kind of a place we're staying in?"

"I think so," Felicia answered calmly.

"I just found out." Rosetta exhaled sharply. "It's run by a religious fanatic!"

Her gaze searched the other faces at the table.

"She won't allow dances here. Not even a square dance. And there aren't going to be any Sunday polo matches or anything."

If she expected an explosion, it failed to materialize.

"We knew that before we came," Felicia told her, smiling to take the edge from her words. "In fact, Miss Duncan would not have made arrangements for us to come out here if Mrs. Chandler weren't a Christian."

"You see," Joan put in quietly, "Felicia and I have given our hearts to God too. We are Christians."

"Well, I can tell you this much! I'm going to call Dad the first thing in the morning and tell him that I'm coming home! I'm not going to stay up here and–and fossilize!"

CHAPTER 3

THE GHOST TOWN

There was a brief silence. Felicia and Joan looked at one another helplessly.

"Shouldn't you give the Lazy Bar Y a chance first?" Joan asked. "Is it fair to leave without finding out whether you like it or not?"

"I knew before I came that I wasn't going to like it." She looked around. "How can you have any fun in a place like this, a thousand miles from nowhere?"

"A great many people spend a lot of money every year to come out here," Felicia reminded her. "They wouldn't come if they didn't like it."

"Just name one thing there is to do around here that's interesting and exciting," the girl challenged. "Just name one."

"Horseback riding," Sherry suggested.

Rosetta shrugged her shoulders.

"I have two horses of my own back home, and I've ridden so much I'm utterly bored with it."

"Have you ever done any mountain climbing?" Joan asked her. "That's great sport."

The girl shivered just at the thought of it.

"I can't even look down a flight of stairs without getting dizzy."

She allowed her voice to rise, mindful that the guests at the nearby tables were listening to her.

"I'm going to call Dad and get out of this dump just as fast as I can. And you aren't going to talk me out of it."

The waiter came with their dinners. Felicia and Joan bowed their heads in silent prayer. Sherry looked at them and did the same.

For a while after they started to eat, the conversation lagged.

"You know," Felicia said midway through the dessert, "I remember reading an interesting book about the old days here in Colorado. Did you know these mountains are sprinkled with ghost towns that sprang up during the gold rush days?"

Interest gleamed in Sherry's eyes.

"The people all moved away," Felicia went on, "but these ghost towns are still standing."

By this time even Rosetta was listening intently, though she masked her interest with a scowl.

"Wouldn't it be fun if we could find one of those old towns and go through it?" Joan put in.

"There wouldn't be anything like that around here," Rosetta scoffed.

"They used to do a lot of gold mining around here," Felicia said. "Aunt Abigail told us that."

A brief silence settled over them.

"You know," Joan said, "I was looking at that old map of this area that's hanging in the lounge. There are some names of towns on it that I've never seen before."

As they left the dining room, Joan led them over to the old map.

"Just take a look at this. There are two or three towns that must have been in existence then but aren't now."

They studied the map with growing interest.

"Calumet City," Sherry said, pointing. "Now that's close by. It even looks as though it's on Lazy Bar Y property."

She turned to face her companions.

"Wouldn't it be fun to ride up there and explore it?"

"I was just going to say the same thing," Joan replied.

Rosetta was interested in spite of herself.

"There's probably nothing up there now," she said.

"We could go and find out," Felicia commented. "It ought to be an interesting ride anyway."

Rosetta and Sherry walked back to their cabin.

"We'd better turn in," Joan said. "I just realized how bushed I am."

"I think we ought to talk to Aunt Abigail first."

They found the ranch woman in the dining hall visiting with some of the guests.

"Certainly," she said in answer to Felicia's question about going up to old Calumet City. "It's all right for you to ride up there. I don't think there's anything there that would give you trouble. It's just an abandoned gold mine and a few dilapidated old buildings."

She went over to the map with them.

"I don't think there's any danger of getting lost," she continued. "Here are the ranch buildings. Our property is bound by the creek on one side and a barbed wire fence on the other. All you have to do is find the gate at the far end of the grazing land. There's a well-traveled trail from there up to Calumet City. It used to be part of the old road. I'm sure you can manage it without difficulty."

The girls met for breakfast the next morning and went out to the corral where one of the hands saddled horses for them.

Rosetta examined her mount distastefully.

"I thought we were going to have horses," she remarked. "I didn't know they were going to be refugees from a glue factory."

"Don't you be complaining, Miss," the cowboy said, eyes twinkling. "These here broncs aren't much to look at, but if you give them time, they'll get you where you're going."

They went northwest across the parched pasture-land, through the gate, and up the narrow, twisting road to the deserted old town.

The girls got their first peek at Calumet City through the trees. They reined in silently, looking at the scene before them. It was a scrawny, ramshackle, paintless town with the hush of decay over it. A town of broken windows, sagging roofs, and the litter of a century of emptiness.

Rosetta's throat tightened, and she swallowed uneasily.

"I–I really don't think there's anything to see in those buildings, do you?" she asked hesitantly.

"I wouldn't miss this for anything," Joan said, shuddering happily. "I'm all goose bumps now, and we aren't even there yet."

Felicia glanced Sherry's way.

"You really don't think anyone's living up here, do you?" the other girl asked.

"Aunt Abigail would have told us if there had been," Felicia replied.

"Maybe she doesn't know anything about it," Rosetta put in.

"Now that's a horrible thought if I ever heard one," Joan observed.

They loosened the reins, and their horses moved forward slowly.

"Calumet City must have been quite a town at

one time," Felicia said. "Look how wide the main street is."

No one answered her.

At the first store building, she dismounted and tied her horse to a crumbling hitching rail out front.

"Are we sure we–we want to go in?" Rosetta asked.

"We can't go back without going in some of the buildings," Joan told her. "We'll be the laughingstock of the ranch if we don't."

"We'd be a *live* laughingstock anyway."

Felicia led the way up the half-rotted boardwalk to the door. The glass had long since been broken out, and one of the hinges was missing, so the door swung outward at the bottom.

Felicia pushed the door, and it creaked open with the protesting squeal of metal against metal.

Joan gasped aloud.

"Joan!" Sherry cried. "Don't do that!"

"I–I'm sorry," Joan stammered.

They stepped inside and looked around. Dust lay in thick layers over everything. It hid the color of the counter and covered the name on the side of the nail keg in the corner.

"Someone has been here," Felicia said, indicating tracks on the floor.

"Rats," Rosetta said shuddering.

They crossed the rough pine floor to the back door, dust billowing up as they walked.

"Well," Joan said at last, "there's nothing here. We'd just as well be on our way."

They left the building and walked over to the next. It, too, was in a sad state of disrepair.

"It's just about like the other one," Sherry observed.

"Isn't it terrible to think of a town dying this way?" Rosetta said. "It gives me the creeps just to think about it. All of the people who used to live here are gone now – just like that."

"The people who built Calumet City must have worked as hard as those who started any other town," Sherry continued, "and what good did it do them? There isn't even a town left. It makes life seem empty and meaningless, doesn't it?"

"Life is empty and meaningless," Felicia answered, "unless we settle things with God. Unless we confess our sin and put our trust in Jesus to save us."

"What do you mean by that?" Sherry asked.

The muscles in Rosetta's face stiffened, and belligerence leaped to her eyes.

"She's just trying to preach to us," she murmured as she turned and walked briskly to her horse.

"You can stand here all day if you want to," she said curtly, "but I'm going over and have a look at that gold mine."

Without giving anyone a chance to say more, she rode to the mine at the end of the main street, and the others followed a dozen paces or so behind.

"Are any of you going with me?" Rosetta asked as she dismounted.

"Now wait a minute," Felicia protested. "We can get into trouble going into a place like that."

"Nobody's going to care," Rosetta went on.

There was anger in her every movement. She left her horse, reins dangling in approved western fashion, and strode purposefully to the mine shaft.

Joan looked Felicia's way.

"We can't let her go down there," she whispered. "We've got to stop her."

"But how?"

Joan had no answer.

Rosetta went in the first door and stopped uncertainly. Her companions came up behind her.

"What's the trouble?" Felicia asked.

"The outside door was open," Rosetta said, "but look at this. Somebody has locked this inside door."

Felicia and Joan sighed their relief.

"Then we won't be going down in the mine," Joan said.

Rosetta still stood there, shaking her head.

"But why would anyone want to lock a mine that doesn't have any gold in it?" she asked.

"We can ask Aunt Abigail about that later," Joan answered.

"I certainly will," Rosetta muttered, her forehead wrinkling with perplexity.

The girls stopped at a grassy spot along the road

and ate lunch before riding back to the ranch. Just inside the gate, Joan veered to the right, in the opposite direction from which they had come that morning.

"Now where do you think you're going?" Felicia asked.

"Aunt Abigail told us about a beautiful little mountain stream that borders the Lazy Bar Y pasture on this side. I'd like to see it."

"Sounds like a good idea," Sherry put in.

"I've had all the riding I want for one day," Rosetta said, the corners of her mouth drooping.

Nevertheless she rode along with them.

After a ride of some twenty minutes or more, they reached the place where the creek adjoined the Lazy Bar Y property line.

Felicia reined in.

"Aunt Abigail told us about the stream," she said, "but she didn't say anything about a fence."

Sure enough. Someone had put a heavy fence between the ranch pastureland and the mountain stream.

And then Joan noticed the old creek bed some forty or fifty feet inside the new fence line. A quick look upstream revealed a newly erected earthen dam that shunted the water to one side and down into a new creek bed.

"And look at those cattle!" Rosetta exclaimed. "They're trying their best to get to water."

Felicia and Joan had seen the cattle as they first

rode up, pushing against the fence and bawling plaintively, almost a hundred of them. But somehow the situation did not come into focus until that very moment.

"Who would do a thing like that?" Felicia asked of no one in particular.

Joan's temper flared.

"I don't know who would do a thing like that," she said, dismounting with sudden resolve, "but I know who's going to knock it down so those cattle can get water!"

She went over to the fence and took hold of one of the posts, trying hard to shake it.

"Here," Rosetta said, coming up beside her, "let me help."

"I wouldn't do that if I were you!" spoke a voice that was harsh and rasping.

The girls looked up quickly to see a lean, hard-faced rider staring at them from across the ravine.

CHAPTER 4

WATER RIGHTS

The girls glared indignantly across the fence at the rider.

"Who gave you the right to put up this fence?" Rosetta inquired hotly.

The man leaned on the saddle horn and laughed, showing his tobacco-stained teeth.

"I don't reckon we have to have permission," he informed her with maddening politeness. "In this country, a person can do as he pleases with his own water."

"But just look at those cattle!" the girl continued with a wide sweep of her arm. "They're about to die of thirst. They've got to have water!"

"That's not my worry," he said. "I've got my own problems."

"But–but that's not human!" Rosetta spluttered. "You can't leave those cattle without water."

"There's plenty there for everybody," Felicia said. "You can't possibly have enough cattle to use all of it."

He straightened in the saddle.

"How do you know how much we can use?" he demanded. "If you're so worried about those cattle, you just turn around and go tell Mrs. Chandler that her cattle are thirsty and need a drink. That's her concern. Not ours!"

"But you have no right to put up a fence like that!" Joan answered.

"We did it just the same." His voice grew louder. "Now you'd better turn those horses of yours around and start for the Lazy Bar Y lodge before I get my dander up and come over there and spank you."

Rosetta put her hands on her hips.

"You wouldn't dare!" she exclaimed defiantly.

"Come on, girls," Felicia said softly. "It isn't doing any good to talk to him. Let's go and see Aunt Abigail."

"Now you're being smart," the man called after them.

They rode off at a brisk canter.

Still boiling, Rosetta glanced over her shoulder.

"I've never heard of anything so cruel! We should have stayed there and torn that fence down so those cattle could drink! There isn't a court anywhere that would do anything to us, even if he did have us arrested! That's absolutely brutal!"

"That would only have caused more trouble," Joan said. "The thing to do is to let Aunt Abigail handle it."

They rode into the yard, their horses lathered and breathing heavily. Mrs. Chandler had seen them coming and hurried out to meet them.

"What is it?" she wanted to know. "What's happened?"

Hurriedly they told her what had taken place.

"And," Rosetta concluded, the words tumbling out fast, "those cattle are so thirsty they're almost crazed. And that–that so-called man was just sitting across the stream watching them!"

Aunt Abigail's voice was firm enough, but her eyes darkened with concern.

"There must be some mistake," she said. "I'll have to go over and see Norris and Will Jennings."

"Go over and see them?" Rosetta echoed. "What good is that going to do? I thought you'd have your foreman, or whatever you call him, take some men and knock that fence down. That's the only thing to do. It's not human to let those cattle go without water."

Aunt Abigail managed a half-hearted little smile.

"I'll be back in a little while."

The girls stood in the yard until her ancient truck had rattled out of sight.

"I certainly hope she's able to get something done over there," Felicia mused.

"Talking isn't going to do any good," Rosetta announced. "We saw that a little while ago. The only thing they'll understand is action. I still think she ought to have that fence torn out. That would show them!"

"Aunt Abigail can't do that," Joan said quickly.

"I don't know why not."

"In the first place, it wouldn't be Christian."

Rosetta looked at her and at Felicia intently.

"Just what do you mean by that?" she asked. "Is it Christian to let those cattle suffer the way they're suffering now?"

"Of course not," Joan answered. "But the Jennings brothers put up that fence. Aunt Abigail doesn't have the right to go over there and tear it down, even to water her cattle. If the fence shouldn't be there, then it's the sheriff's job to see that it's removed."

"It doesn't make sense to me."

"We can't take the law into our own hands," Felicia tried to explain, "even to accomplish something good. And it isn't Christlike for us to do something wrong in order to accomplish something that's good, like getting water for those cattle."

"But what if it takes a long time?" Sherry wanted to know. "What will Mrs. Chandler do for water then?"

"We'll have to pray that it won't take long," Joan said.

"A lot of good that will do," Rosetta muttered, her voice rising with her temper. "If you ask me, I don't think much of a religion that will keep a person from doing something to stop all those cattle from dying of thirst."

The girls supposed Aunt Abigail would be gone for several hours, but before they had fed and watered their horses, the truck was back. Mrs. Chandler got out slowly, closed the door, and stood motionless for an instant or two.

Rosetta ran toward her.

"Did everything go all right?" she asked.

But there was no need to ask the question. Aunt Abigail's face was ashen, and the lines in her forehead seemed to have deepened. One glance revealed that things had not gone right at all.

"I'll tell you all about it in a minute or two," she said, walking toward the door of the foreman's house. "Mr. Weaver will have to send men to bring in those cattle for water."

The tall, muscular ranch foreman listened intently while she told him what had taken place.

"But they had no right to fence off that water!" he exclaimed hotly. "No right at all! The water rights to that stream have always belonged to the Lazy Bar Y!"

"We'll have to get it straightened out as soon as we can, Mr. Weaver," Aunt Abigail said evenly. "But in the meantime, we've got to get those cattle where they can be watered."

He eyed her solemnly.

"I can tell you this much, Mrs. Chandler," he said, his voice dry and expressionless, "we've only got one good well on the place. And it's not going to last long under that sort of drain – unless it rains and rains soon."

She breathed deeply, and it seemed to Felicia that for the first time her voice faltered.

"I know."

When Mr. Weaver and three cowhands were gone after the cattle, she turned and retraced her steps to the truck where the girls were standing.

"I suppose you heard what I told Jess Weaver," she said.

"We didn't mean to be eavesdropping," Felicia told her, "but we have been very much concerned."

"That's quite all right. I want you to know."

She breathed deeply.

"Dwight Chandler – my husband – always told me that his grandfather had filed for the water rights to the entire stream at the time he first bought the Lazy Bar Y. He did it to keep the water free. When he died, he put it in his will that water was not to be denied anyone as long as there was any available. Everyone around here has known that."

"Then the Jennings brothers had no right to put up that fence," Felicia said. "You can force them to take it down."

Frowning seriously, Aunt Abigail raised her eyes.

"That's the thing I can't understand," she began. "Norris and Will Jennings claim they've got the water rights to the stream. They say they just filed on them. They say they have a legal right to put up the fence in order to keep us from using the water. They told me I could check at the courthouse if I didn't believe them."

"But that can't be!" Rosetta exclaimed. "The first water rights would have priority. Everybody knows that."

"That's the way it seems to me too," Aunt Abigail answered. "But it's something we've got to get straightened out."

She sighed wearily.

CHAPTER 5

THE MYSTERY DEEPENS

The following morning, shortly after breakfast, Aunt Abigail went to Ridge Corners to check the records in the courthouse. She had invited the girls to go along.

"I'm concerned about those cattle," Rosetta said after a time. "Did they get watered?"

"Oh, yes," Aunt Abigail answered. "They were brought up to the well near the barn."

The girl's lips narrowed.

"I couldn't help overhearing what Mr. Weaver said about the well," she went on. "What are you going to do if the well goes dry before this matter of the water is straightened out?"

Aunt Abigail's face grew granite hard.

"We are going to get it straightened out – in one way or another! That's why we're going to the court-house this morning."

Although her voice rang with determination, the conversation left her pensive and silent. She drove in to Ridge Corners, stopped at the post office, and got out before she spoke again.

"I'll only be a minute," she told them.

Rosetta waited until she was inside the building.

"I still think it's criminal not to tear down that fence so those cattle can get water."

"They're being watered," Felicia reminded her.

"They're getting water now," Rosetta admitted, "but you heard what the foreman said. That well is apt to run dry any time. What are they going to do then?"

"It's something to pray about," Joan told her.

The answer startled Rosetta. She surveyed Joan questioningly.

"If I were Mrs. Chandler," she said, "I'd do a lot more than that."

Before anyone could say more, Aunt Abigail came back to the truck, sorting through a handful of mail. A smile came to her face.

"Well," she said, getting into the truck, "it looks as though things are looking up for the Lazy Bar Y in one department, at least. We have quite a few new reservations."

"Do you have a letter for me?" Rosetta wanted to know.

She recognized the handwriting on the envelope Mrs. Chandler handed her and squealed with delight.

"It's from Dad," she exclaimed. "I knew he'd be writing before long."

She tore open the envelope and read the letter hurriedly. While she did so, Mrs. Chandler began to open the reservation letters.

"Dad still says he's coming out here," Rosetta announced, looking up from the letter she was reading, "but I know he's not going to like it at a prehistoric place like the Lazy Bar Y. He's got to have some excitement!"

She spoke impetuously, staring at Aunt Abigail.

But Felicia noticed that her threat to leave was conspicuously absent.

"If Dad were here," Rosetta continued, "he'd *make* you do something about that water!"

Mrs. Chandler looked at her watch.

"I am going to have to hurry to get the business at the courthouse attended to before noon," she said. "You girls can go with me, or you can look around town, just as you please."

"We want to look around town, don't we, Sherry?" Rosetta asked.

"It would be fun to go into some of these quaint little stores."

Felicia and Joan turned to the ranch woman.

"We'll go with you," Joan said. "That is, if you'd like to have us."

Aunt Abigail's smile flashed reassuringly.

They went to the office of the county clerk together.

"And what can we do for you, Abigail?" the clerk asked amiably, strolling over to the desk.

"I've got a real order for you this time, Joe," she answered. "I'd like to look at the records for 1883 or 1884."

"1883?" he repeated, frowning. "Why so far back, Abigail? That was before either you or I were born."

Her smile was infectious.

"I've got my reasons."

He hesitated momentarily.

"I'm sorry, but no can do."

Worry lines in her face deepened.

"You mean you don't have them?" she asked.

"To tell you the truth, we don't have anything before 1899. Sorry."

"But the county was organized before that, I know."

"You're right," he said. "It was organized before 1899, but that doesn't help us any, Abigail. Our records don't go back any farther."

"Are you sure?"

His face became even more serious.

"You know I've been in this office for twenty-eight years," he continued. "If our records went back any farther, I'd surely have found them by this time. There's not a nook or a cranny in this old courthouse that I haven't been in. Those early records just aren't here. And as far as I know, they never have been."

He noticed the dismay on her face.

"Is it something important?"

"Yes, Joe," she said, "it's something very important. I'm having some trouble over the Lazy Bar Y water rights."

Joe leaned forward, resting his arms on the desk.

"You know, I was afraid something like that might be brewing," he said, "when that new guy came in to file for the water rights on that stream that runs 'twixt you and the Block 8. I told him Grandpa Chandler had those water rights and had left it in his will that no one should be denied any water for stock or personal use as long as there was any. But it didn't make any difference."

"I tried to tell them the same thing," Aunt Abigail went on, "but Norris and Will Jennings both claim that Grandpa Chandler didn't file for water rights to the stream. They said they'd had it checked. That was the reason they filed and got them."

The county clerk straightened and forced himself to look at her.

"I couldn't do any different, Abigail," he said. "If I could, I'd have done it because I know what's right; and I know how things have been out there for all these years. But sometimes the law makes a person do things he doesn't like to do. We checked all the records we had here and couldn't find that any had been filed for the Lazy Bar Y. So they had a legal right to file."

She sighed deeply.

"That's what I was afraid of."

Her great weariness was apparent in every move as she turned away. It seemed as though the information had drained all the strength from her body.

"Thank you, Joe," she said over her shoulder in a voice that was scarcely audible. "Thank you very much."

"If there's anything I can do, Abigail–" he said helplessly.

She scarcely heard him.

Felicia opened the door, and Mrs. Chandler walked down the stairs. It was not until they were outside that either of the girls spoke.

"I'm terribly sorry," Felicia said. "If only there was something we could do to help."

"Isn't–isn't there something that can be done?" Joan asked.

Aunt Abigail paused on the street corner.

"I can't understand it," she began hesitantly. "I can't understand it at all. Grandpa Chandler was a very careful man and a fine Christian. He would not have lied to everybody. He never would have told us that he had filed on the water if he hadn't."

"That means the water rights must be recorded in those old books," Felicia said.

Aunt Abigail nodded.

"Wherever they are."

"Don't you have any record of it at home?" Joan asked. "Any papers that would prove he had filed for the water rights?"

"I don't know whether there ever were any papers," she replied. "The old ranch house burned down in 1904 or so, and nothing was saved."

"But there's got to be something you can do," Joan said firmly. "Do you have any plans?"

Dejectedly she shook her head.

"I don't know," she said. "I just don't know."

They went to the grocery store for supplies, picked up the other two girls, and headed back to the Lazy Bar Y.

Felicia and Joan noticed the bright glitter in Rosetta's eyes, the excited flush on her cheeks, and the smile that played now and again on her so-often-surly mouth. Aunt Abigail noticed too.

"My, but you look thrilled, Rosetta," the woman exclaimed. "What did you do? Find a new boyfriend?"

"What makes you think I'm so thrilled?" she demanded.

"I know girls, my dear. Something happened today to put a sparkle in your eyes."

She glanced over her shoulder.

"Perhaps you'd better let the rest of us in on it."

"Then it wouldn't be a secret anymore."

At the ranch, Rosetta and Sherry clambered out of the truck and hurried toward their cabin, whispering to one another excitedly.

"I wonder what's got into them," Felicia said.

At that moment, the ranch foreman came riding up on his big gray cow horse.

"Did you find out about those water rights, Mrs. Chandler?" he asked abruptly.

She was slow in answering.

"I found out," she admitted, "but it wasn't good news. Joe tells me they have actually filed for the water and have legal right to it. It belongs to them."

"But it can't be!" he exploded. "Everybody knows that Grandpa Chandler had the water rights to that stream. And they all know that he made arrangements to have it kept open and free to everyone."

"I know all of that," she answered, "but there just aren't any records to prove it."

Jess Weaver's face showed anger.

"There's no law against taking back what's rightfully ours," he said. "There's never been a fence to keep Block 8 cattle from that water, and there's not going to be any fence to keep ours out! I'm not going to let that fence stop me! I'll take a few of the boys out tonight, and we'll take care of things. But good!"

"Oh, don't do that!" Aunt Abigail ordered quickly. "You will have to bring the cattle up to the well again. We aren't going to have trouble over that water."

"But it's yours, Mrs. Chandler. You know it and so do I and everyone else around here! All the neighbors will be with us on this thing!"

"I won't have it any other way," she said in a firm voice. "We'll have to keep the cattle up near the well until it rains."

The foreman stared at her.

"It's your ranch," he said, resignation in his voice, "and they're your cattle. I can't tell you what to do. But I can tell you this much. If they were mine, I'd see that they got water if I had to go over with a crew of men and knock down those fences to do it."

"That," she reminded him decisively, "is against the law."

He sighed deeply.

"We can bring the cattle up, I suppose. But this well's not going to stand pressure like that indefinitely. What are you going to do when it goes dry? Answer me that!"

But there was no answer in her troubled eyes.

CHAPTER 6

ACCUSED!

Felicia and Joan went over to the lodge for dinner at the usual time, but Rosetta and Sherry were not there. Joan swept the dining room with a glance.

"I don't see them," she said. "Should we wait?"

"I think Aunt Abigail would like to have us wait," Felicia replied.

They crossed to a sofa before the huge, rustic fireplace and sat down.

"I only wish there were more we could do to help her."

"This cattle trouble doesn't look very good, does it?" Joan remarked after a time. "What do you suppose Aunt Abigail will do if she can't get water from the stream and the well goes dry?"

Felicia shook her head.

"Mr. Weaver seems to think that's going to happen, and soon."

"I just can't understand it," Joan went on. "There is plenty of water in that stream for all the cattle of both ranches. Why would the new owners of the Block 8 be so mean?"

Felicia drew in her breath slowly.

"I wish we knew the answer to that," she said. "If we did, I have a hunch we'd be a long way toward working things out."

In a few minutes Sherry and Rosetta entered the room, party dresses rustling as they walked.

"My," Joan exclaimed appraisingly, "I didn't know the dinner was formal!"

Rosetta giggled.

"There are a lot of things you don't know."

She pulled out a chair and sat down grandly.

"What is it?" Felicia asked. "A surprise party?"

"This," Sherry explained smiling, "is Saturday night."

Joan and Felicia looked at one another questioningly.

"And what's so special about Saturday night?" Joan asked.

Condescendingly, Rosetta smiled.

"Saturday night is – well, Saturday night."

"We'd like to take you with us," Sherry apologized. "In fact, we talked about asking you but decided it wouldn't do any good. You wouldn't go anyway."

"Not that it would hurt you any," Rosetta added, smiling again.

"If you're talking about a dance," Felicia said, "you're right. We wouldn't be interested in going."

Rosetta turned to her almost belligerently.

"And why not?" she asked. "What's so bad about dancing?"

Felicia's mouth firmed as she searched for words.

"I used to ask the same question before I became a Christian and put my trust in God," Joan broke in. "I argued that dancing didn't hurt me any, so I was going to dance."

"That's just the way I feel about it," Sherry said defensively. "Exactly."

"Then I saw that it did hurt me in a lot of little ways. When I came home from a dance, I found it almost impossible to read my Bible and pray. It seemed as though there was a barrier between God and me."

The smile left Sherry's face, and she looked away.

"Then," Joan went on, "I began to see that God expected certain things of me as a Christian. He expected me to present my body as a living sacrifice to Him and even to keep away from the very appearance of evil. It wasn't long until I saw that it applied to dancing as well as to a number of other things. So I quit."

"But a person has to have *some* fun," Sherry countered.

"We do," Felicia assured her. "To be honest with you, I have more fun now than I ever did before I gave my heart to Christ."

"I certainly haven't missed dancing either," Joan said.

"Well," Rosetta replied, shrugging her shoulders, "you have your fun, and we'll have ours."

Sherry looked at her uneasily.

The waiter came with their dinners, and when he was gone, Rosetta changed the subject. It seemed to Felicia that Sherry was unnaturally quiet during the meal. She and Rosetta finished eating as quickly as possible and left with two young married couples who were also guests at the Lazy Bar Y.

"Don't wait up for us," Rosetta called out, waving her hand.

Felicia put a lump of sugar in her tea and stirred it carefully.

"I can't help feeling sorry for them," she said.

The next morning Felicia and Joan went down for breakfast at the usual time, but Sherry and Rosetta were not in sight.

"I suppose they're still in bed," Joan said. "I didn't hear them come in, but it must have been awfully late."

Felicia looked at her watch.

"Aunt Abigail told me that a retired minister who lives up the mountain always comes in for a Sunday morning service. I hope Sherry and Rosetta don't sleep late enough to miss that."

"If Rosetta knew about it, she would," Joan observed.

The girls were just finishing breakfast when their friends came into the dining room.

"Well," Rosetta murmured, "I thought the least you would do was to wait breakfast for us."

"We thought you would probably sleep until noon," Joan told her.

Rosetta dimpled provocatively.

"I felt like it, for a fact."

She sighed.

"But, oh, did we have fun! It was really wonderful! You should have been with us!"

Sherry's eyes met Felicia's. For an instant, they were held there.

"Did you enjoy yourself?" Felicia asked.

Sherry swallowed hard and her gaze lowered.

"I–I guess so," she answered without enthusiasm.

"Everybody had a wonderful time," Rosetta continued. "You should have been there."

Felicia and Joan remained at the table while the other girls ate their toast and drank their coffee. They were just finishing when the bell sounded to start the service in the lounge.

"What's that for?" Rosetta asked suspiciously.

Felicia told her.

"I certainly don't feel much like going to church this morning," she grumbled.

"I'm sure you'll like it," Felicia said. "Aunt Abigail says that Mr. Larimore is most interesting."

"And," Sherry added, "it won't last very long."

Rosetta seemed indifferent.

"I suppose I'd just as well go," she said. "I'm out of bed now, and it will give us something to do in this dull joint."

Although only a handful of the guests at the Lazy Bar Y were Christians, most of them gathered in the lounge for the church service. They sang two hymns, accompanied at the piano by Mrs. Chandler, and Mr. Larimore got up to speak.

He was a robust, broad-shouldered individual, gray of hair, but young of eye and step. And his voice was vibrant and alive.

His message was simple but hard-hitting, and Rosetta squirmed uneasily under its impact. Felicia caught the troubled look in her eyes and prayed in silence.

The service ended all too soon, and the people began to file outside. Joan turned to their guests.

"What did you think of it?" she asked.

Rosetta's voice was cold and hostile.

"I should have stayed in bed."

Sherry said nothing at all. She kept her eyes averted so that neither Felicia nor Joan could read them.

As Felicia and Joan passed the desk, one of the couples who had accompanied Rosetta and Sherry to the dance the night before was paying their bill.

"You have reservations for another week," Aunt Abigail reminded them gently.

"You aren't telling me anything," the man retorted

curtly. "But we've had all we can take of this lousy place. We're spending the rest of our vacation where we can have some fun!"

Aunt Abigail shook her head sorrowfully.

During the afternoon, Joan and Felicia watched for Rosetta and Sherry as they mingled with the other guests in the lodge and around the grounds. But the two girls avoided them carefully. It was not until dinner that evening that they were all together again.

Rosetta's eyes were bright and hard, and her mouth was set in a firm line.

"I've lived through one Sunday," she sighed, "but I don't know whether I could live through another or not. I swear this is the dullest place I've ever been in my life."

Sherry brushed a hand across her forehead.

"Does anyone have an aspirin?" she asked. "I've got a beastly headache."

Rosetta fumbled in her purse.

"What did that church service do to you anyway?" she demanded. "You've had a headache ever since it was over."

Sherry pushed back from the table.

"If–if you'll excuse me, I think I'll go to my cabin," she said. "I feel terrible."

Before she could leave, a large green car drove up to the lodge and a tall, well-dressed stranger in western clothes got out and came striding up the steps.

"Who's that, Sherry?" Rosetta whispered.

She settled back in her chair.

"I think we saw him at the dance last night, didn't we?"

"That's what I was thinking, but I can't figure out who he is."

By this time the stranger had stepped inside the screen door and was looking around, anger in his dark eyes.

In a moment, he spied the girls and came over to them.

"Can you tell me where Mrs. Chandler is?" he demanded.

Aunt Abigail got to her feet and went over to him.

"Good evening, Mr. Jennings," she said, holding out her hand.

"Jennings?" Joan whispered under her breath. "He's one of the owners of the Block 8, isn't he?"

Felicia nodded.

Sherry and Rosetta stared at one another.

"The Block 8!" Sherry exclaimed. "Why, that's where we went to the dance last night."

Color leaped to Rosetta's cheeks.

"We didn't know the owners were the ones who were keeping Lazy Bar Y cattle from getting water," she said, "or we'd never have gone there!"

She fell silent as the tall intruder spoke again.

"Mrs. Chandler," Jennings muttered, "this time you've gone too far!"

She stared at him curiously.

"I don't believe I follow you," she said without raising her voice.

"Don't try to play so innocent with me! I know what you did! You had Weaver and your hands knock down that fence tonight so your cattle could get to our water!"

"I did nothing of the kind, Mr. Jennings," she countered. "I gave orders to Mr. Weaver to bring the herd to the well for water."

"You can't make me believe that! Anybody knows that well of yours wouldn't last more than a couple of weeks with a strain like that on it."

"I've told you the truth, Mr. Jennings."

He drew himself up haughtily.

"You have until noon tomorrow to get those cattle off our land and get that fence put back!" he almost shouted. "And if it happens again, Norris and I will sue you for every dime you've got!"

Before she could protest further, he turned and stalked noisily out of the dining room and down the steps to his car. An instant later, he went roaring away.

The color drained from Mrs. Chandler's face, and her lips trembled.

CHAPTER 7

BRIBERY WORKS

For an instant or two, Mrs. Chandler remained motionless in the middle of the dining room. Her hands worked nervously as she stared after the car that had long since disappeared from view. Then she tucked nervously at a strand of hair and moved mechanically toward the door.

"Poor Mrs. Chandler," Sherry whispered.

"I wish I were a man!" Rosetta muttered. "I wouldn't let him get away with that! He knows she didn't order her cow hands to tear down his fence. He's just being mean!"

Felicia stood up quickly.

"Excuse me," she said. "I'll be back in a few minutes."

"Where are you going?" Joan asked.

"With Aunt Abigail."

She caught up with the ranch owner as she reached the walk outside the lodge.

"Aunt Abigail," she said, "I want you to know that we're very sorry for you."

Mrs. Chandler took Felicia's small hands between her work-worn hands and squeezed them tenderly.

"Thank you, my dear."

It was a moment before Felicia could speak.

"And I wanted to tell you that Joan and I are praying for you."

The smile came to Aunt Abigail's face again.

"I was confident of that," she said.

They walked along the narrow, gravel lane toward the ranch foreman's little house. Neither spoke, but Felicia knew instinctively that Aunt Abigail was glad she was along.

"Do you think Mr. Weaver really tore down the fence so the cattle could drink?" Felicia asked after a time.

The ranch woman was a long while in answering.

"I know he felt that the Jennings brothers were unjust," she said, "and he was angry enough to tear down the fence. But I don't think he would deliberately disobey my orders. He's never done that before."

Jess Weaver invited them inside.

"That Jennings!" he exclaimed angrily. "He's a rancher. He knows why that fence went down. He just wants to cause us some trouble."

Aunt Abigail peered at him questioningly.

"What do you mean?" she asked.

"He knows those cattle were so thirsty they pressed against the fence until it went down."

The wrinkles in Weaver's forehead deepened.

"We've been trying to keep them from the stream, Mrs. Chandler," he went on, "and we've been trying to keep them from the well as much as possible too. We've got to try and make that well last until it rains. Jennings knows that, and he knows that when cattle get crazed with thirst they're powerful hard to keep from water."

He sighed deeply.

"We'll have to move them out the first thing in the morning," she said, "and rebuild the fence."

He nodded.

"But that's rough, Mrs. Chandler. That's awful rough to stand by when you're herdin' critters that are so thirsty they'll do most anything to get water."

Felicia saw the hurt in his eyes.

He exhaled slowly.

"I tell you, if we don't do something about that water pronto, or if it doesn't rain before long, our well's going dry. Then we will be in for it!"

Mrs. Chandler and Felicia said goodbye and stepped outside.

They walked slowly.

At the lodge, Aunt Abigail stopped.

"Thank you, Felicia," she said softly. "Thank you for everything."

Instead of going back to the building, she went across the yard to the big ranch house.

Felicia went inside where the girls were waiting for her. Sherry was still there in spite of her headache.

"What happened?" Joan wanted to know.

"Nothing." Felicia sat down. "Aunt Abigail just told Mr. Weaver to move the cattle the first thing in the morning and get the fence fixed."

"I don't know what's the matter with that man!" Rosetta exclaimed. "I wish Dad were here! He'd fix that–that Mr. Jennings."

Most of the tables in the dining room were empty, but the girls did not leave.

"Sherry and Rosetta have just been telling me something very interesting," Joan said in a low voice. "Why don't you tell Felicia too?"

Sherry rubbed her throat in a quick, nervous gesture.

"Well," she began, "it's as we told you when Mr. Jennings came in. We were at the Block 8 last night to the dance. We saw the advertisement for it in town when we went with you and Mrs. Chandler."

Felicia nodded.

"I rather imagined that was what happened."

"I thought it was going to be so much fun," she went on, her voice faltering, "but I've been miserable ever since I went."

"But that's not what Joan is talking about," Rosetta broke in quickly. "The thing she was interested in was the fact that Mr. Jennings gave the Stewarts a week's free vacation if they'd leave the Lazy Bar Y and go over to the Block 8 ranch."

"That's why they went," Joan said. "It wasn't because they found it so dull here."

"Hmm, that's strange," Felicia said. "That's very strange."

"And," Joan went on, "what's even stranger is the fact that he made the Stewarts promise not to tell Mrs. Chandler why they were leaving."

"And the Stewarts let it slip," Sherry said, "but they really didn't think we'd say anything to Mrs. Chandler about it."

Felicia and Joan glanced at one another.

"Then the real reason Mr. Jennings and his brother gave the Stewarts a free vacation was to get them away from the Lazy Bar Y."

"In other words," Joan whispered, "they know Aunt Abigail is having financial trouble and they want to do everything they can to make it worse."

"But that seems so cruel," Sherry countered.

"Anybody who would do what they did to those cattle," Rosetta said, "isn't going to care about anything."

"That's what I figure," Joan continued. "First of all, they got their hands on that water. The next thing they did was to put up a fence so the Lazy Bar Y couldn't water their cattle. And all Aunt Abigail has is the foundation herd she'll need to replenish the ranch. If she has to sell them, she'll be ruined."

"And," Felicia added, "now they're trying to get the tourist business away from her."

She paused and took a deep breath.

"But why?" Joan put in.

"Maybe," Sherry suggested, "they just don't like Mrs. Chandler."

"I suppose that could be," Felicia said, "but I don't really think that's it. There must be some other reason. Some big reason!"

The silence was deafening.

"That," she said, "is something we've got to find out."

The girls looked at one another breathlessly.

"But how?"

CHAPTER 8

WHAT NEXT?

As usual, Felicia and Joan had their devotions together that night. Joan read from the Bible and each girl prayed.

"We want to remember Sherry in prayer tonight," Felicia said. "She was really disturbed by the service this morning."

"She seemed to be terribly under conviction about that dance," Joan added.

Felicia nodded.

"I wanted to talk to her this afternoon, but I couldn't. She and Rosetta avoided us most of the day."

"She doesn't want to talk to us."

"I'm going to try again tomorrow."

They went to bed, but had a difficult time getting to sleep. They both rolled and tossed restlessly.

After what seemed to be an hour or two, Joan rolled over on her side and raised up on an elbow.

"Felicia," she whispered softly, "are you asleep?"

The other girl opened her eyes.

"Not yet."

"Neither am I."

She breathed heavily for a short time.

"Whenever I close my eyes I see those cattle piled up along that fence trying to get to the water."

Joan sat up.

"I don't see how those Jennings brothers could be so cruel."

"And worse yet," Felicia said, "there isn't anything that can be done about it. They've got the law on their side."

"I'm not so sure," Joan answered. "The law is supposed to hand out justice, and it certainly isn't just for them to fence off that water from Lazy Bar Y cattle when Grandpa Chandler let everyone else have water freely all those years."

"I know all that."

Felicia swung her feet over the side of the bed and sat up.

"I keep wondering why they're doing that," she said, speaking slowly. "I don't know anything about ranching, but I do know they've got more water in that stream than they can possibly use. They couldn't carry enough cattle on the Block 8 ranch to drink it all, and there wasn't any evidence that they were going to use it for cultivation."

"That's been disturbing to me too. Why would

they spend the money to put a dam across the stream and divert it over to their land?"

"We keep asking ourselves that question," Felicia continued, "but we don't come up with any answers."

She lay down again, but it was a long while before she finally drifted off to sleep.

The next morning, Felicia and Joan sought out Aunt Abigail and told her what Sherry and Rosetta had said about the Stewarts leaving.

"I'm not surprised," she said. "I'm not surprised at all."

"Just why are they doing all these things?" Joan asked.

The lines in Aunt Abigail's forehead grew deeper.

"I've asked myself the same question a hundred times."

The girls went into the lounge with her and sat down in one corner.

"Some unidentified party is trying to buy the Lazy Bar Y," the ranch woman went on. "A real estate agent was out to see me last week. I rather suspect it is Will and Norris Jennings, but I'm not sure."

"That could be the reason for all this," Joan said.

"But if they want to buy the ranch," Aunt Abigail observed, "why would they want to force me to sell off the foundation herd? They would have to rebuild, too, when the drought is over."

"Maybe they think that is the only way they can get you to sell," Joan suggested.

"That might be," Mrs. Chandler admitted, "but there are so many questions. Why would they insist on buying the Lazy Bar Y when there are half a dozen other ranches in the neighborhood that can be bought for half of what they're worth?"

She looked from one girl to the other.

"For that matter," she continued, "why would they want to buy another ranch at all? They just got the Block 8 a few months ago, and they don't have enough cattle on it now to make it pay off."

She looked at her watch and got quickly to her feet.

"I suppose we should go in for breakfast," she said. "It's getting late."

There was a brief pause.

"I was just wondering if you girls would like to go to town with me this morning?" Aunt Abigail asked. "I've decided to see an attorney and find out just what rights I have."

Sherry and Rosetta appeared at the door. Felicia looked at them significantly and then at Joan.

"Why don't you go to town with Aunt Abigail, Joan?" she asked. "I think I'll stay at the ranch this morning."

Joan and Aunt Abigail left the Lazy Bar Y in the noisy truck after breakfast and drove to Ridge Corners.

"I called Mr. Dodson this morning," Mrs. Chandler said, stopping before a small brick building, "and he asked me to meet him here at nine o'clock."

Even as she spoke, a thin, waspish individual came

bustling up the walk, a briefcase under his arm. He unlocked the door and disappeared inside.

A moment later Aunt Abigail and Joan were in his office, seated across the desk from him.

The ranch woman told her story calmly from the very beginning.

"And so," she concluded, "I decided to see you, Henry, and find out exactly what rights I have."

He picked up a small paperweight and toyed with it for a minute or two before speaking.

"I wish I could give you more satisfaction than I can, Aunt Abigail," he said affectionately. "Everyone around here knew that Grandpa Chandler had filed for water rights to the stream in the name of the Lazy Bar Y. Or at least we all assumed he had."

"He had the water rights," Aunt Abigail broke in. "I'm convinced of that."

"So am I, in my own mind," he replied, "but unfortunately we need proof. I know there are some older records than we have in the courthouse, but unless we can find them, there's not a thing we can do."

Paling noticeably, Aunt Abigail clutched the arm of the chair until the cords stood out on the backs of her hands.

"But what could have happened to those records?" Joan broke in. "If he had filed for the water rights, that filing would have to be recorded somewhere, wouldn't it?"

The attorney nodded.

"Yes," he answered, "but so many of our early day records are incomplete – especially in this county."

"Why here?" Joan asked.

Mr. Dodson chuckled good-naturedly.

"I remember hearing my father tell about the big battle they had when the courthouse was moved from Calumet City to Ridge Corners."

"That seems to be a strange thing to fight about," Aunt Abigail commented.

"It was an important matter," the attorney went on. "Calumet City was the logical county seat until the mines closed and people began to move away. When the rest of the county wanted the county seat at Ridge Corners, the few people left at the mine town were bitter about it. They knew it would mean the death of Calumet City if it happened. So the fight got awfully bitter."

"It seems that I remember Grandpa Chandler telling something about it shortly after Dwight and I were married," Aunt Abigail said.

"All the old-timers had stories about that battle," Mr. Dodson continued. "It was a snorter. Some of the people who lived up at Calumet City stole the records from the courthouse and hid them after they lost the election. They never were able to find some of them."

"That could explain why Grandpa's water rights aren't on file," Aunt Abigail remarked.

"That's exactly what I think."

"Do you suppose there's any chance of finding them?" Joan asked.

"Well," the attorney replied, "I suppose there's always a possibility. But if you could find them, you'd be doing a lot better than anyone else has. Some people swear they've been burned."

"If they had been put away somewhere, they'd surely have been found by this time," Aunt Abigail said, masking the concern in her voice with a smile. "Would it be possible to get someone to testify that Grandpa Chandler had actually filed for the water rights? Isn't there something we can do along that line?"

His lips narrowed.

"If we had someone who could swear that he had actually seen the old records and could testify to that effect, we might have a chance in court; but even then, it would be a battle."

The attorney shook his head.

"That happened so long ago none of the people who might have seen it are still alive. No, I'm sorry, but I'm afraid there's nothing else we can do."

"Thank you, Henry."

"I–I'm sorry, Aunt Abigail. I wish there was more I could do."

Her smile came back, wan and pale, but a smile, nevertheless.

"Thank you, Henry," she said again. "Thank you very much."

Joan took her arm as they walked out to the truck. For a moment, Aunt Abigail leaned heavily on her, as though her weariness almost overwhelmed her. Joan's heart ached as she looked at her.

"Do you think it would be possible to find those old records?" she asked.

"I'd like to think so," she replied, "but Henry is right. If they hadn't been destroyed, someone would have found them long before this."

"Do you think it would do any good for Felicia and me to ride up to Calumet City and see if–if we can find anything?"

Aunt Abigail laid a hand on Joan's arm.

"It's sweet of you to want to help me," she said, "and I'd be so grateful if someone could find some sort of proof that would force Norris and Will Jennings to let us have water. But I don't see how it could happen."

"You don't mind if we go up there, do you?" Joan persisted.

That drew a smile.

"Of course not, Joan. If you'd like to."

The girl lapsed into silence. If only they could find something that would help!

* * *

Back at the Lazy Bar Y, Felicia and the other two girls finished breakfast leisurely and went into the lounge to send messages.

"I've got to write to some of the guys in our group of friends back home," Rosetta remarked with a toss of her head. "They all made me promise."

"I owe Mom a letter," Felicia told her.

It was almost as though she had not spoken, for Rosetta continued breathlessly.

"I'm going to have to make up something to tell them. I'd just *die* if they knew what sort of a prehistoric sanitarium Dad sent me to."

"But that's lying," Felicia reminded her gently.

"What's the diff?" Rosetta shrugged her shoulders. "They'll never find out."

She started for her cabin.

When Rosetta was gone, the two girls sat down across from one another.

"I feel so sorry for her," Felicia said. "She thinks her life is so full, but it's so empty. So very empty."

Sherry's eyes darkened.

"What makes you say that?"

Felicia looked up.

"Do you think she's happy?" she asked. "Really happy?"

"She says she is."

"But how could she be?" Felicia continued. "She thinks only of herself and having a good time."

Her eyes sought Sherry's and held them fixedly.

"Could you be happy living that way?" she asked.

Sherry started, and her lips trembled slightly.

"I–" she began.

The words trailed away dismally.

Felicia noticed that and prayed for wisdom.

"You seemed terribly disturbed by the message yesterday, Sherry," she began. "Joan and I couldn't help noticing how quiet and preoccupied you were the rest of the afternoon after Mr. Larimore spoke."

Embarrassment was evident in the girl's face.

"The only way to be truly happy," Felicia went on, "is to get this matter of the way you're going to live settled with God. You know, He has a blueprint for our lives. All we have to do is realize we're sinners and need a Savior and then put our trust in Him."

Sherry tried to look at Felicia, but her gaze wavered uncertainly. Not, however, before Felicia saw the hurt leap to her eyes.

"I'd like to help you, Sherry."

"Please!" Her voice was harsh. "I've got a frightful headache."

She got to her feet and moved away.

"Won't you excuse me?"

Though there was a question in her voice she did not wait for an answer. She turned quickly and, rubbing a hand over her forehead, walked noisily across the lounge to the outside door.

Felicia followed her to the door and watched until she had gone into her cabin.

* * *

It was two or three hours later that the truck returned to the yard. Felicia went out to meet it. Aunt Abigail stopped, her hand on the truck door. For an instant, she looked sharply at Felicia.

"What is it?" she almost whispered. "Is something wrong?"

"I didn't realize it showed," the girl said, trying to smile.

"What is it, Felicia?" Joan wanted to know.

She forced herself to smile.

"It probably isn't as bad as I make it," she answered. "I'm just a little down this morning. But another couple pulled out an hour or so ago."

Aunt Abigail flinched as though she had been struck.

"Who was it?"

"I don't remember the name," Felicia went on, "but they had reservations for a month."

"Did they say why they were leaving?" the ranch woman asked.

"Their answer was about the same that the Stewarts gave you," she replied. "They said it's so dull here they couldn't stand it another minute."

They went into the ranch house before Aunt Abigail spoke again.

"We've tried to have a varied program," she said more to herself than to her younger companions.

"We've had organized rides, camping trips, mountain climbing, swimming, tennis, and shuffleboard."

"That isn't the sort of thing they were talking about," Felicia went on. "They wanted some excitement. Something like the Saturday night dances over at the Block 8 or gambling."

"We wouldn't have either one," Mrs. Chandler said firmly.

* * *

Although Felicia and Joan did not see Sherry for the rest of the afternoon, the girl came down to dinner at the usual time and sat with them. She was quieter than usual and carefully avoided Felicia's gaze.

"We've just got to do something to help Aunt Abigail," Joan said, telling the other girls what had taken place that day. "She just can't carry on alone."

"It would be easy if Mrs. Chandler wasn't so narrow and bigoted," Rosetta replied. "Everybody likes to dance. She could get a band, have a Saturday night square dance, and the guests would look forward to it all week."

"She would never do that," Felicia answered.

"There are plenty of things to do here," Joan said. "Aunt Abigail has a full program of entertainment."

"Entertainment?" Rosetta shuddered. "You can call it entertainment if you want to, but I call it dull. D-u-l-l–dull! People want some excitement, like a dance or a polo match."

"Or a rodeo," Joan put in off-handedly. "A Saturday afternoon rodeo."

She straightened slowly, turning the matter over in her mind.

"That's not a bad idea, even if I did have it."

Rosetta looked at her.

"Where would we get the riders?"

"We wouldn't need too many. There are the men who work the ranch."

"Only a couple of them are real riders," Rosetta scoffed. "I don't think the others could stay on a horse three jumps."

"We could still have a rodeo," Joan continued.

"Aunt Abigail has always got *me*."

The other girls stared at her.

"You?"

"What's so funny about that?" Joan demanded. "I can ride."

"And just what can you ride?" Rosetta demanded.

"Most anything. Aunt Abigail's truck, a bronc, a Brahma bull."

Rosetta laughed.

"You on a Brahma bull? You make me hysterical."

"Don't get so worked up," Joan countered. "I've always wanted to ride a bull."

The man at the next table leaned over to her.

"Now that, young lady," he said, "is something I'd stick around all week to see."

Joan's face went ashen.

"Ride a Brahma?" she echoed. "What have I been saying?"

CHAPTER 9

BACK AT THE GHOST TOWN

A light shone in Felicia's eyes.

"I think that's an excellent idea, Joan. You'd be the star attraction."

"I'm sure people would like that better than a dance," Rosetta said. "If it goes over, maybe you could do it every Saturday afternoon."

"And if it goes real well," Sherry added, "Mrs. Chandler might like to have you ride Wednesday afternoons as well."

"Now listen, girls," Joan spoke quickly. "You can go ahead and have your fun if you want to. But you know I didn't mean that about riding a Brahma bull. I was just talking."

Felicia looked at the others.

"It sounded real to me," she said. "What did you think?"

"You repeated it four or five times," Sherry told her, "in front of everybody."

"But you all knew I was joking."

She looked from one to the other seriously.

"Joking?" Rosetta echoed. "It didn't sound like a joke to me."

"You know I wasn't serious, Felicia."

"All I know is that you've always told me how resourceful you are. As far as I'm concerned, this is just more evidence of Bailey skill and ingenuity."

"Just wait until I get you alone!"

They finished eating and sauntered outside, intending to go for a walk, when they met Aunt Abigail and Jess Wheeler, the ranch foreman.

In the growing darkness, Felicia saw the concern in the woman's face.

"Is everything all right?" she asked. "There isn't more trouble?"

Aunt Abigail shook her head.

"Not exactly. There's just more of the same old trouble." She breathed deeply. "Another couple is pulling out day after tomorrow. They just gave notice."

"Was it for the same reason?" Joan asked.

Aunt Abigail nodded.

"They're going to spend the rest of their vacation somewhere else," they said.

"We were trying to think of something to give the excitement some of the people want," Felicia offered. "Have you ever thought of a Saturday afternoon rodeo? It seems that almost everyone is interested in rodeos."

Aunt Abigail turned the matter over in her mind.

"What do you think, Jess?"

"It might be all right," he said. "The hands we've got now aren't the same sort of riders we used to have, but I think we could work out something – if you think it would help."

"I don't suppose it would hurt to try," Aunt Abigail remarked without enthusiasm.

"You don't know about your star attraction, Aunt Abigail," Felicia said. "Joan has volunteered to ride a bull."

The ranch woman's eyes opened wide.

"A–a bull?"

"A Brahma bull," Rosetta exclaimed. "Don't you think that's a stunning idea?"

Joan colored.

"You know I was just joking," she answered.

Jess Wheeler looked at her curiously.

"Now there," he said, "is a great idea. That's an attraction neither the Block 8 nor any other dude ranch can imitate. You let the word get out, Mrs. Chandler, and you'll have the Lazy Bar Y packed out. We could probably pick up some extra money selling tickets."

"Now, Jess," Aunt Abigail scolded, "we don't want to tease Joan."

"Who's teasing anyone?" he asked. "I'm serious.

That's a great attraction. Just the thing to put the rodeo over."

"But I–" Joan stammered.

"Don't give it another thought, Miss," the foreman said gallantly. "I'll take care of everything."

Joan stood motionless.

"Why did I have to open my big mouth!"

The girls said nothing to anyone about the coming rodeo, but someone must have been talking, for all the guests seemed to know about Joan's prospective ride.

One of the men stopped her in the lodge.

"I've done a little riding myself, young lady," he said in mock sincerity. "If you'd like to get some pointers on Brahma bull riding, I'm just the person to talk to."

Joan's face colored.

"Thank you," she stammered, "but I think I know all I'll ever need to know about Brahma bulls or–or any other breed."

The stranger laughed good-naturedly.

"Don't get so worked up about it. Relax! The first dozen bulls are the hardest."

Rosetta and Sherry came up just then.

"You were right, Joan," Rosetta said. "Everybody's excited about the rodeo. It's going to be the biggest thing the Lazy Bar Y has ever done."

"We're so excited we can hardly wait," Sherry said.

Joan swallowed hard.

"N-n-neither can I."

"I'll tell you what we'll do," Rosetta went on. "We want to be helpful. We'll talk to Jess Wheeler and see if he'll find an old bull. One that can't jump around very much."

Felicia joined them in the lodge.

"You know, Joan," she said keeping her voice low, "with all the excitement about the rodeo, I'd forgotten to ask what you and Aunt Abigail found out at the attorney's office."

"It doesn't look good," Joan answered, repeating what Henry Dodson had said. "There doesn't seem to be anything Aunt Abigail can do unless those old records turn up."

"I was afraid of that." Felicia exhaled slowly. "Isn't there anything that can be done?"

Joan glanced around and leaned forward until they could hear her faint whisper.

"I've been thinking about it," she said. "The chances are those records didn't leave Calumet City. I think they're still hidden up there."

"If they weren't burned," Sherry countered. "You mentioned that some of the old-timers think they were destroyed."

"What would be the purpose of destroying something like that? It surely wouldn't do any good."

"Unless," Rosetta added, "it was someone like the Jennings brothers who could gain by it."

Joan's forehead knitted.

"I think we ought to go up to Calumet City and look around."

"That does sound exciting!" Rosetta exclaimed.

The next morning, before leaving to ride up to the old ghost town of Calumet City, the girls sought out Aunt Abigail to ask about the lock on the mine.

"We thought maybe it was locked to keep people out," Rosetta said.

"It is," Aunt Abigail answered, "but not because of any gold in there. The mine played out years ago. My husband was afraid the old timbers might give way and trap someone in there if he left it open. I suppose that padlock has been on for twenty years."

Rosetta could not conceal her disappointment.

They saddled their horses and rode up the mountain to Calumet City. The trip seemed to be shorter than before.

"I wonder how long it's been since anyone has been here?" Felicia asked, looking around uneasily.

"Not too long ago," Joan replied. "Look at all those horse tracks! Someone has been riding up here!"

Rosetta's gaze searched the area frantically.

"Do you suppose someone's here now?" she asked in a whisper.

Felicia dismounted and studied the tracks with great care.

"No," she said at last, "these tracks are a day or two old."

They followed them for several minutes.

"It hasn't been too long since we were up here,"

Joan answered laughing. "Maybe we're following the tracks of our own horses."

"That would be a good joke," Sherry said.

"But we stopped at several of the buildings," Felicia reminded them. "These tracks go down the middle of the street. They were made by another party."

"Well," Joan replied, "I'm not going to worry about it now. I'm just glad someone was here a couple of days ago."

"Maybe it was the Jennings brothers looking for those old records," Rosetta suggested.

Felicia frowned at her.

They rode to the first intersection and reined in.

"Now," Sherry asked, "where do we start?"

"Where is the old courthouse building?" Joan asked.

"I don't think the records would be there," Felicia said. "Do you? Mr. Dodson told you about the big fight to move the courthouse to Ridge Corners. The first place any thieves wanting to steal the county records would look would have been in the courthouse. They'd have been found if they had been hidden there."

"I suppose you're right at that," Rosetta said. "But where do we look?"

Joan started suddenly.

"Look down there!" she cried.

"Now what's the matter with you?" Rosetta demanded.

"There's someone on the trail below!" Joan stammered. "They're coming this way!"

CHAPTER 10

ON THE RIGHT TRACK?

Fear gripped Felicia, and she gasped aloud. Sherry took hold of her arm with trembling fingers.

"Do–do you see anything?" she whispered.

Felicia looked down the trail, trying to see between the trees and pick up the sight of riders headed up to the deserted mining village.

"I–I don't see a thing," she spoke at last.

Rosetta came up beside her, lips parted slightly. Her face had gone ashen, and she was shivering involuntarily.

"Neither do I," she stammered.

"You really must be jumpy, Joan," Felicia said. "There's nothing down there – I hope."

"But I'm sure I saw someone on horseback," Joan countered. "In fact, I thought I saw several riders just below that turn."

They all stared at the area where she pointed.

"There's nothing there now," Rosetta announced, her courage returning. "If we're going to look around, we'd better get at it."

"If someone would come riding up," Sherry stammered, "I think I'd die of fright."

"We don't have anything to worry about," Rosetta answered, a smile at the corners of her mouth. "We've got two such good Christians along that nothing will happen to us."

"As a matter of fact, I've been praying for our safety ever since Joan thought she saw someone coming," Felicia said, "and I'm sure Joan has too."

Rosetta turned in her saddle to look at them.

"Mrs. Chandler has been praying too," she answered, "and she's such a good Christian she won't even let her guests dance. And what's happened to her? God certainly hasn't answered Mrs. Chandler's prayers, has He?"

"She still has the ranch," Joan replied, "and she still has her herd. I have faith that everything is going to be all right for her, regardless of how black things look right now."

"God doesn't promise to give us an easy life," Felicia added. "Nor does He promise to remove all our trouble. He does promise to save us from the results of our sin if we put our trust in Him, and He promises to help us and give us strength to take what comes if we call on Him."

Sherry flushed. She grasped the saddle horn and looked down.

"And," Joan put in pointedly, "I can tell you from experience that living for God is the only way to true happiness."

Sherry flinched.

"Can't you talk about anything else?" she blurted angrily. "All I've heard out of you two since we met is religion–religion–religion. I'm sick of it."

Even Rosetta was shocked by the explosion. It was reflected in her face.

"I–I'm sorry you're offended, Sherry," Felicia said. Truly I am. We've only wanted to help you."

"Then leave me alone!" Sherry's lips trembled with emotion, but she did not continue.

Tears came into her eyes and began to roll down her cheeks. Then, slumping forward, she began to sob convulsively.

Her companions stared at her helplessly.

"Well!" Rosetta exclaimed, turning on Felicia and Joan with mounting indignation. "You've got Sherry all upset over this stupid religion of yours! Are you satisfied now?"

It was several minutes before Sherry lifted her head.

"I–I'm sorry," she managed.

Rosetta cast a meaningful glance at Joan and Felicia.

"You have nothing to be sorry for," she said.

Sherry's tortured eyes met Felicia's and held there momentarily. "If we're going to get out of here before dark, we'd better hurry," Rosetta kept on, digging her heels into her horse's flanks.

"Where do we start?" Sherry asked. Her eyes were still red from crying and her voice shaky and uncertain.

"I still think the mine is the first place we ought to look," Rosetta replied.

"But we can't go in there," Joan protested. "It's locked. And besides, there's danger of falling timbers."

"We could tell whether the timbers are rotten or not before we go in," Rosetta answered. "We wouldn't have to go in any place where we would get into trouble. Besides, those record books might be close to the door."

Felicia tugged at the lobe of her ear thoughtfully.

"That padlock has been on there for twenty years," she said. "It probably wouldn't be too difficult to break the lock and get in. And, of course, it wouldn't be like breaking and entering. The mine belongs to Mrs. Chandler, and she wouldn't care if we went in."

"The only reason it's padlocked is to keep someone from getting hurt," Rosetta went on. "She told us herself that the mine is worthless."

They rode up to the mine and dismounted. Joan and Rosetta entered the outside door together.

There was a short silence.

"That's strange," Joan muttered.

Felicia and Sherry pressed close and looked over her shoulder.

"What is it?" Felicia wanted to know. "What's so strange?"

"It's just an ordinary padlock," Rosetta observed. "If that's what you're talking about."

"I know that," Joan answered. "But Aunt Abigail told us that her husband put it on twenty years ago."

"What about it?"

"Take a look at it, will you?" she said, holding up the padlock between her thumb and forefinger. "The lock itself is rusted but look where it rested against the door latch. It's bright and clean!"

Rosetta stared at her.

"What does that prove?"

"Maybe nothing," Joan answered, "but it seems if that padlock had been in place for twenty years, it would all have rusted."

"That's true," Felicia said. "That padlock isn't rusty enough to have been there very long."

"Maybe your dear Mrs. Chandler isn't as good a Christian as you think she is," Rosetta commented. "Maybe she lied to us."

Felicia and Joan both shook their heads vigorously.

"No," Joan said, "she wouldn't have lied to us. Somebody else must have put that lock in place, and Aunt Abigail doesn't know anything about it."

"Or," Felicia added, "her husband might have changed it just before he died."

"Well," Rosetta complained, "we're not going to solve anything standing out here. If we're going to look for those records, let's do it. If we're not, let's get started back to the ranch. This place is giving me the shivers."

Sherry nodded. Her face was still white and drawn, and she looked as though she would burst into tears again at any moment.

They left the mine area and walked to the nearest building, leading their horses. Rosetta surveyed it uneasily.

"Do you suppose it's safe to go inside?" she asked.

"Safe or not," Joan remarked, "if the rest of you go in, I'm going too. I'm not going to stand out here alone."

Felicia stopped, her hand on the doorknob.

"All set?" she asked.

The door might have been locked a long while before, but the latch had been broken and the door stood half ajar.

The girls reluctantly went up on the steps behind her.

"I don't want to go in," Sherry managed. "But I don't want to miss anything."

"It gives me goose bumps just to think about exploring a place like this," Joan said, "but they have the strangest fascination for me."

"If they ever f-f-fascinated me, it–it's g-g-gone now," Rosetta stammered.

Felicia walked across the floor, peering intently into every corner of the general store.

The shelves were empty and half broken out, and cobwebs laced diagonally from one to the other. A thick coat of dust covered everything in sight.

For a brief instant, there was no sound in the deserted building. Then a rat poked his nose cautiously around the counter and went scurrying across the floor.

Rosetta screamed.

"That was just a rat," Joan told her.

"Just a rat?" Rosetta echoed. "I'd as soon be around a snake."

"Well, he's gone now," Felicia said in her calmest, most matter-of-fact voice.

She continued to move forward. In spite of the calmness of her voice, her heart hammered fiercely, and her mouth went dry.

"I don't think the record books would be in this old store building," Rosetta said, edging toward the door.

"We'll never know unless we look," and Felicia went on.

They moved slowly around the deserted store. Vandals and thieves had already been there years before and left their calling cards in broken windows and furniture that had been ruined. Although they went through the two rooms carefully, they found nothing.

As they left, Joan paused in the doorway.

"Now where do we go?" she asked. Although she

tried not to show it, her weariness and despair were apparent.

"We've been to this building and the mine," Felicia told her. "Why don't we go through the store next door and keep that up until we've visited them all?"

"Sounds like a good idea," Sherry said.

"If we don't see any more rats," Rosetta added.

The next building was almost an exact duplicate of the one they had just left. And so was the next and the next. They made their way down the north side of the short street, crossed over and started back.

"And we still haven't found anything," Joan said a few minutes later.

"What's more, we won't find anything either," Rosetta murmured. "We're just wasting our time."

Felicia took a tissue from her pocket and wiped the grime from her face.

"It won't take long to look in one more building," she said. "And that's all we've got left."

Sherry moved toward the door.

"We can't quit without checking it too."

They left the store and walked over to the only two-story building still standing in Calumet City.

"This must have been a hotel," Felicia exclaimed, glancing around the small lobby.

As usual, the windows and furniture were broken, but the unusual wooden desk in one corner remained.

"This must have been where the people regis-tered," Joan said.

Felicia poked around in the dust behind the high counter.

"What's this?" she exclaimed aloud.

"What's what?" Rosetta asked, pushing closer.

Felicia lifted a stack of heavy books to the top of the desk.

Joan's eyes widened.

"Do you suppose they could be the lost record books?" she asked incredulously.

Felicia opened the cover of one.

"Oh!" she cried out in dismay. "Just the hotel registry."

"I told you we wouldn't find anything," Rosetta complained.

"Just a minute," Joan said suddenly. "Let me look at those other books. A hotel wouldn't have such a stack of registration books."

She took one of the books from the bottom of the stack and looked at it. For an instant she stared at the faded page.

"Felicia!" she cried, her voice taut and trembling. "This may be what we're looking for!"

The girls crowded around, staring at the old journal.

"Can you figure out what it is?" Sherry asked.

They were so engrossed they heard nothing until the door to the building was swung open and someone stepped inside.

"What are you doing here?" a harsh voice demanded.

CHAPTER II

DISAPPOINTMENT

"**M**r. Jennings!" Joan exclaimed as she grasped Felicia by the arm.

The tall rancher peered at each of them in turn, his face full of anger.

"What are you doing here?" he demanded.

Then his eyes lighted momentarily on Sherry.

"I know you," he said. "You were over to the Block 8 to a dance one Saturday night."

Flushing hotly, Sherry nodded.

"You don't have to look so guilty about it." He laughed genially. "You aren't the only Lazy Bar Y guest who gets fed up with a steady diet of old lady Chandler's so-called Christianity and comes over to our place to kick up her heels."

Sherry's cheeks blazed, and she looked down quickly.

"That must be an interesting hotel register," he observed.

The girls did not answer him.

By this time, half a dozen others crowded into the old hotel, talking and laughing excitedly.

"Thought I'd bring some of the guests from the Block 8 up to have a look-see at a real ghost town," Norris Jennings explained.

The Block 8 guests swarmed upstairs and, an instant later, called to Mr. Jennings.

"I'll be with you in a jiffy," he responded.

He turned to confront Felicia and Joan once more. The humor in his eyes died, and the corners of his mouth tightened.

"If I were you girls," he warned, "I'd stay away from Calumet City."

Joan smiled impishly.

"But we like it here."

"You can get in trouble in a place like this." He hesitated significantly. "And if you do, there's no one to help."

"I think we can take care of ourselves all right," Joan protested.

He laughed mirthlessly.

"Some of these old buildings are built over abandoned mine shafts," he said, "and these wooden floors are getting rotten. I wouldn't want one of you to get hurt."

"We'll be careful," Felicia assured him.

He moved closer, and his harsh voice lowered.

"Just stay away from here! Then you won't be hurt!"

He glared down at them, then turned and clomped noisily upstairs.

"Come on," Rosetta whispered; "we'd better get!"

Joan glanced at the books on the desk, left those that had served as a hotel registry and picked up the other two.

"He saw what we were looking at," Sherry whispered. "What if he noticed that we took some of them?"

"That's a risk we've got to take!"

They hurried out to their horses, mounted them, and went briskly down the street toward the trail.

No one dared to speak until they were half a mile from Calumet City. Felicia half turned in the saddle to see if Norris Jennings and his party were coming.

"I wonder if these books are part of the old county records," she mused, her grip tightening on the volume in her hand.

"We can't stop to look now," Rosetta said. "It's going to be dark in a little while. That means they'll be coming back before very long. We can't waste any time on the way!"

Joan leaned back in the saddle and propped her book against the saddle horn. Holding it with one hand, she opened it to a page near the back.

"We might have known it," she muttered in dismay. "This book is the record of the hotel expenses."

Felicia did the same with the book she was carrying.

"The back of this one seems to be like the one you've got," she said, "but the front isn't."

She frowned momentarily.

"It's something about land and deeds and–" Her throat tightened, choking off the words.

"Felicia!" Joan cried, tensing in the saddle. "Maybe we have found something!"

"We'd better not stop here to talk about it," Rosetta said nervously. "That Mr. Jennings and his friends aren't far behind us."

Felicia glanced back and saw that the Block 8 party was less than a mile behind them.

Rosetta kicked her horse into a brisk trot and held him there. The other three did the same.

"Just think," Felicia mused after a time, "if we've got the book with the Lazy Bar Y water rights recorded in it, all of Aunt Abigail's troubles will be over."

"Right now," Rosetta answered, "I'm interested in our own troubles. And they're right behind us."

Although Norris Jennings and his guests traveled the same trail most of the way back to the Block 8, they did not draw any closer to the girls.

"It looks as though we're going to make it," Joan said when they were close enough to see the lights in the lodge.

"I was beginning to wonder," Rosetta put in. "I don't think I've ever been so glad to get back to the Lazy Bar Y as I am tonight."

When they rode into the ranch yard, a portly,

gray-haired man came to the door of the lodge and peered into the darkness. Rosetta reined in suddenly.

"Dad!" she squealed with delight. "Oh, Dad! You did come!"

She almost leaped from her horse and ran to throw herself into his arms.

He hugged her affectionately.

"I couldn't stay away any longer."

"I'm so glad you're here," she repeated over and over again. "I'm so glad you're here."

After she introduced the girls to her father, Felicia and Joan went off to their cabin with the books under their arms.

"Now," Joan whispered, "to see if we've found what we're looking for."

She switched on the light and locked the door. Felicia sat down on the side of the bed and opened the grimy volume. Wrinkling her nose distastefully, she glanced at her fingers. They were smudged with dust.

"These must be county records of some sort," she said hesitantly.

Joan sat down beside her.

"They are!" she exclaimed. "They're tax records."

Felicia's forehead creased deeply.

"They wouldn't have water rights recorded in a tax book, would they?"

"I wouldn't think so."

Felicia thumbed the pages mechanically.

"That's all these are," she said. "Tax payments."

She looked up.

"What I can't figure out," she went on, "is how we came to find these books so easily when people have been looking for them for years."

"Look where we found them," Joan said, "almost in plain sight but mixed in with the hotel registry books. Other people probably saw them a hundred times and figured they were just old hotel records."

Felicia sighed.

"I feel terrible. When we saw that we had some sort of a record book, I was sure we'd found what we've been looking for."

Joan got up and walked across the room listlessly.

"And," she said, "while we're doing all of this looking, the water supply is getting lower every day."

She faced Felicia.

"What's Aunt Abigail going to do?"

* * *

They were getting ready for bed when there was a timid knock on the door. The girls both started.

"Who is it?"

"It's me, Sherry." Her voice was tense and wavering.

"Just a minute."

Felicia opened the door.

Sherry stepped inside. Her face was drawn, and her eyes were swollen.

"I'm sorry to bother you like this," she began,

crossing to a chair and sitting down. "But I had to see you tonight. I couldn't put it off any longer!"

Felicia and Joan waited patiently.

"I don't know whether you realize it or not," Sherry continued in faltering tones, "but once, a long time ago, I confessed my sin and put my trust in God."

"Once in a while you said something that made me think you might be a Christian," Felicia told her.

"I was going to live a good, Christ-honoring life," the girl went on.

She swallowed hard.

"Then I began to let the world creep into my life until–until I–"

The tears came again, and she could no longer continue.

Felicia put an arm around her shoulders.

"You don't need to tell us about it, Sherry," she said. "Tell it to God."

"But–" Sherry raised her head, eyes pleading desperately. "But I can't live a Christian life. I'm just too weak."

"None of us can lead a Christian life by ourselves," Joan said. "And I ought to know. I surely tried hard enough."

She lowered her voice.

"Then I discovered that God doesn't expect us to live a Christian life in our own strength."

"He doesn't?"

"He knows how weak we are," Joan went on.

"That's why He gives us so much help. He gave us the Bible to tell us how to live. He gave us the church and Sunday school and youth groups to instruct and guide us. He gave us Christian friends to encourage us. And then He promises to help us Himself if we will call on Him."

Felicia got her Bible and went over a number of those wonderful promises with Sherry. At last, they knelt together.

CHAPTER 12

A GOOD LEAD

The next morning when Felicia and Joan went into the dining room for breakfast, Rosetta and her father were already there.

"Dad got me up at a beastly hour to go horseback riding with him," Rosetta complained, glancing at him affectionately.

"You said yourself that sunrise was well worth it," he countered.

"Oh, it was, but I'll have to have toothpicks to prop my eyes open before night."

"How do you like it here, Mr. Bloom?" Felicia asked after a time.

"I'll tell you more about that a little later," he answered.

"Dad feels just as I do," Rosetta broke in, "that it's the dullest, most devastating, prehistoric place he's ever been."

Mr. Bloom smiled tolerantly at his daughter.

"Suppose you let me speak for myself, my dear."

They were just giving their orders when Sherry came in, her face radiant.

"Now what's happened to you?" Rosetta demanded. "Did you meet a new boy or something?"

Sherry smiled mysteriously.

"Or something," she replied.

"If it's that good," Rosetta continued, "let us all in on it."

Sherry's face grew serious.

"I've been wondering how I could tell you, Rosetta," she began, selecting her words with care. "You see, I've been a Christian for quite a long while. But I drifted away because I found so much enjoyment in the things of the world."

Rosetta paled slightly and tried to laugh, but her laughter was feeble and mirthless.

"When Felicia and Joan started talking to us, I knew I wasn't living the way a Christian should. That's why it bothered me so much."

"It didn't bother me any," Rosetta countered, tossing her head defiantly.

"The service last Sunday after you and I went to the dance the night before was bad enough," Sherry told her, "but when Felicia and Joan talked to us again yesterday, I knew I couldn't go on any longer. Now all of that is behind me."

Her smile broke through again.

"With God's help, I'm going to live the way a Christian should!"

"If that isn't going to be dull!" Rosetta exploded. "I don't know how I can stand it here now without anyone to have a good time with."

She looked at her father.

"Honestly, Dad, this has been the dullest place I've ever been! We don't have to stay, do we?"

His face was thoughtful.

"I told Mrs. Chandler we would be around for a couple of weeks," he replied gently.

The silence was short. Rosetta picked up her knife and transferred it to the other side of her plate. Her lips parted.

And then she laughed defiantly.

"Well," she announced in a hard voice, "I've stood it this long. I guess I can make it another two weeks. By that time. Sherry, you'll probably have seen how ridiculous this all is."

The conversation was strained during the rest of the meal. Neither Rosetta nor Sherry thought to ask about the old record books.

As soon as they finished breakfast, Felicia and Joan excused themselves and left to find Mrs. Chandler.

"I'm not at all surprised," was her comment when they told her about the books they had found. "Somehow I haven't had much confidence in finding proof of Grandpa Chandler's water rights up there."

Her face was sallow, and her eyes dull with concern.

"It looks as though we won't be needing them, anyway."

"What do you mean?" Joan asked.

"The well is about dry," she said. "Mr. Weaver had to water half the cattle yesterday morning and wait until late afternoon for enough water to seep into the well to take care of the others. Another few days and we won't even be able to do that."

She hesitated and then continued.

"And two more couples served notice that they're leaving the last of the week."

She sighed deeply.

"I just don't see how I can hang on much longer. I'm afraid I'm going to have to sell the Lazy Bar Y."

"Oh, no!" Felicia exclaimed.

A small boy came up to the ranch house just then and looked in through the screen door.

"Aunt Abigail," he said, "Daddy asked if you could come to the house right away. He wants to see you about something."

She got to her feet.

"Jess Weaver wants to talk to me," she explained to the girls. "I'll see you after a while."

Felicia and Joan walked out to the porch with her. When she was gone, Felicia turned to her companion.

"I–I feel so bad I could cry," she said.

Joan went to the side of the porch and peered up in the direction of Calumet City.

"You know, Felicia, we found those books in the

hotel. The hotel owner had been using the back pages of one of them to keep his own records."

Felicia nodded. "But there was nothing in it about water rights, and that's what we've got to find if we're going to help Aunt Abigail."

"I know that."

Her eyes glinted with excitement.

"But if he had one book, wouldn't he be apt to have others around somewhere?"

Felicia stopped short, and for a brief moment she stared at her friend.

"Joan!" she exclaimed. "I believe you've got something!"

"It sounds reasonable to me," Joan went on. "It's the only real good lead we've ever had. We've got to go back up there and see if we can find them!"

"But let's not say anything to Aunt Abigail about it. There's no use in getting her hopes raised in case we don't find anything."

They were just leaving the ranch house when Rosetta and Sherry and several other guests caught up with them.

"Oh, there you are!" Rosetta exclaimed. "We've been looking all over for you. We have news for you, Joan."

"For me?"

"You're the young lady who volunteered to ride the bull, aren't you?" one of the men broke in.

"Me, ride a bull?" Joan's cheeks colored. "That's the most ridiculous thing I ever heard of."

"You can't get out of it that easily. We were just talking to Mr. Weaver. We told him how keen we are on the rodeo. He promised that he'd hold it Saturday afternoon as he agreed."

"And," the other man added, "he promised that he'd have you there to ride a bull!"

Joan swallowed hard.

"You don't really mean that, do you?"

"We've never been more serious in our lives," Rosetta said.

Joan looked from one to the other desperately.

"We thought maybe you'd give us a riding exhibition this morning," someone else said, "so we'd have an idea who'd win. You or the bull."

"I can tell you the answer to that right now," Joan managed.

The others drifted away still laughing, leaving the four girls standing there.

"You've really got yourself into something," Rosetta taunted.

"We've got something else that's more important than that," Joan said.

Hurriedly, she and Felicia told them about the record book and what they proposed to do. Rosetta's eyes widened slightly.

"You mean you want to go back to Calumet City again?"

"We've got to!" Felicia exclaimed. "It's the only chance we've got of helping Aunt Abigail."

"Well," Rosetta said reluctantly, "I suppose I can go, but I don't know whether I want to or not."

"We'll be back by the middle of the afternoon," Joan assured her.

"Maybe."

They saddled their horses and rode across the parched pasture toward the old ghost town.

"I still can't figure out why the Jennings brothers are so anxious to run Aunt Abigail away and buy her ranch," Felicia remarked. "It's almost as though they've got a grudge against her or something."

"The thing that disturbs me," Joan put in, "is that they're going to succeed unless we find those old records."

"I don't know why you're concerning yourself so much about Mrs. Chandler," Rosetta complained. "She's nothing to you."

"She's no relative," Joan said, "or anything like that, but she's a good friend."

"And," Felicia added, "she needs help desperately."

Rosetta shook her head incredulously.

They rode up to Calumet City and stopped before the hotel building.

"Now," Joan announced, "to see if the rest of those record books are here!"

She dismounted, but Felicia remained in the saddle.

"Aren't you coming?"

"I was just thinking," she said. "Norris Jennings caught us up here yesterday afternoon and warned us to stay away from Calumet City. There's a good chance he might ride up this way today to see if we took his warning."

"Now's a fine time to be thinking about that," Sherry murmured shuddering.

"We can fix that easily," Rosetta replied. "We can turn around and go back."

"I was thinking we ought to hide our horses," Felicia said.

Joan nodded her agreement.

They led their saddle horses across the wide street, between two buildings, and behind a big clump of brush that effectively screened them from view.

"This ought to be all right," Sherry said.

"Unless we want to get out of here in a hurry," Rosetta added.

They went back to the hotel building and went inside. For a minute or two, they stared at one another.

"Where do we start?" Sherry asked.

"There weren't any other record books behind the desk," Felicia said, thinking aloud. "And there doesn't seem to be any other place here in the lobby to look."

Joan started for the stairs.

"Maybe they're up here."

"Why don't you and Rosetta look around up there? Sherry and I will go through this floor," Felicia suggested.

Felicia and Sherry went into the room that must have served as a dining room and began their search.

They looked behind the old furniture, pulled out drawers, and opened doors, but there was nothing to be found.

"They're not in here," Sherry observed after a time. "That's for sure."

"We still have the kitchen to go through."

"I've been trying to talk to Rosetta about what happened to me," Sherry said as they shifted their search to the little room at the back of the building. "But it doesn't seem to do any good. She just gets angry."

"Remember how angry you got when Joan and I talked with you?" Felicia asked.

Sherry straightened.

"That's right," she said as she moved over to the back window and looked out.

"Felicia!" she cried in a whisper. "Felicia! There's someone coming!"

The girl flew to her side.

"Norris Jennings!" she exclaimed.

"And the man with him is his brother, Will!" Her voice caught. "And they're coming right this way!"

CHAPTER 13

THE SECRET PLACE

For a brief, terrifying instant, neither girl could move.

"What are we going to do?" Sherry whispered.

"We've got to get out of here fast!"

Felicia ran to the stairway and called to Joan and Rosetta.

"But we're not through up here!" Joan protested.

"Will and Norris Jennings are on their way!" Felicia told them excitedly. "They'll be here in a minute!"

"I knew we shouldn't have come!" Rosetta wailed as she and Joan came charging down the stairs.

Felicia ran to the front door. But she was too late! The Jennings brothers were already riding up to the front of the old hotel.

"We can't go out here!"

She froze temporarily, her entire being quivering.

"What can we do?" Rosetta cried, almost hysterical.

"There's a back door in the kitchen!" Sherry exclaimed. Even as she spoke, she made for it. The others were half a step behind her.

Pitch blackness greeted them as she jerked open the door.

Dismay gripped her.

"This goes down into a basement or a cellar or something!" she gasped. "It doesn't lead outside!"

"Go on in!" Joan cried desperately, pushing her forward. "We haven't got time to worry about that now. Those guys are going to be in here in half a jiffy!"

"But it's dark down there!" Rosetta protested.

"I've got a good flashlight!" Felicia told her.

"Sh-shh-shh!" Sherry warned.

Joan crowded in after the other girls and pulled the door shut. And without a moment to spare!

Already Norris and Will Jennings were in the hotel lobby. Their boots made a noisy sound as they crossed the floor.

"We can't stay here!" Joan objected. "If they open this door, they'll have us all!"

"But I'm not going another foot down into this cellar!" Rosetta whispered. "There—there's no knowing what we'll find down there!"

"You can stay up here if you want to," Joan answered, "but I'm going to get as far from those two as I can, and pronto!"

They forced themselves down the rickety stairs to the floor of the musty old cellar.

Huddled together at the foot of the stairs, the girls listened.

"Do you suppose they'll find us?" Sherry asked fearfully.

"If they notice our footprints in the dust on the floor they can track us right down here," Felicia answered.

Joan's shoulders jerked convulsively.

"That's right!"

Shielding the flashlight with her hand, Felicia switched it on.

Rosetta gasped involuntarily at the sudden stream of light, and her hand flew to her mouth.

"Turn that off!" she managed. "They'll see us!"

"That's a chance we've got to take!"

Felicia moved the light slowly around the small cellar. The yellow beam revealed the debris and neglect of a century. Boxes and boards and broken mining tools were stacked against the dirt walls of the cellar and scattered about the floor.

"What are you looking for?"

"Some place to hide."

Felicia surveyed the entire cellar with care, but there was nothing big enough to conceal them.

"What are we going to do?" Rosetta demanded.

Footsteps sounded on the floor above them.

"Shut off the light!" Joan whispered.

Immediately the flashlight flicked off. Almost at that very instant, the door above them opened.

"Now where do you think you're going, Norris?" a coarse voice demanded. "We've got to get over to the mine!"

"I'd still like to know what those kids were looking at when we came in yesterday. They had some kind of old record book."

"Well, it wasn't the book with the Lazy Bar Y water rights recorded in it. If it had been, old Abigail would have hotfooted it into town and got a court order forcing us to turn that water loose."

"Just the same," Norris Jennings kept on, still standing at the cellar door, "everything's so close to working out that we can't take any chances. By the end of the week, she'll be begging us to buy her out."

"What I can't figure out is how the old mine has been left all these years without someone finding that vein of gold."

Gold!

Joan gasped.

"What was that?" Norris Jennings cried.

"Now what's eating you?"

"Didn't you hear anything?"

There was a brief, tense silence.

"You must've heard the rats. The place is crawling with them!" He moved toward the outside door. "Come on and don't be so jumpy. We've got to get another batch of ore samples."

"I'm going to be sure that was rats!" Norris Jennings exclaimed.

He took a step or two down the rickety stairs and leaned down, moving his light around.

The girls pressed close against the wall directly behind the staircase.

"Come on, Norris! We haven't got all day!"

For answer he came down another step or two. There was a sharp, splintering sound.

He swore savagely.

"What's the matter, Norris?" Will Jennings asked, hurriedly going down to him.

"I broke a board in these stairs," he exclaimed, "and I almost broke my leg!"

His brother helped him to his feet.

"I tell you, there's nothing down here. We've got to get over to that mine and get out of here before those fool girls come nosing around again."

Felicia and Joan pressed back against their companions breathlessly.

At last, the Jennings brothers were up to the top of the stairs, and the girls heard Norris hobble across the floor still cursing under his breath.

"Whew!" Joan exclaimed a full minute later. "That was close!"

"We'd better get out of here!"

"We can't leave now!" Felicia warned. "They're still out there somewhere. They'd catch us for sure!"

"If I get out of here alive," Rosetta affirmed, "I'll never go anywhere with you again!"

"That's what I keep telling myself," Joan said laughing.

Felicia switched on the light once more and moved slowly to the stairs.

"It was strange we didn't break through that board," she murmured.

"We're not nearly as heavy as he is," Sherry reminded her.

Felicia found the broken board and studied it carefully.

"And now what do you think you're doing?" Joan asked.

"I just had an idea."

She reached down and took hold of the board on the bottom step and lifted it up.

"You aren't going to find anything that way," Joan scoffed.

"I don't want to find anything," Rosetta wailed on the verge of tears. "All I want to do is get out of here and get back to the ranch. I should never have stayed in this–this terrible place a single day."

"We'll be going just as soon as we can," Felicia told her. "Right now I think I know where we might find that old record book."

She examined each step carefully, but the boards were all firmly nailed into place.

"See," Joan said, "I knew we wouldn't find anything."

"There's another set of stairs," Felicia went on. "Let's try that."

She led them up into the old kitchen once more.

"Why don't you and Sherry stand watch, Rosetta," she suggested, "while Joan and I try the steps?"

"I still don't see what you hope to find," Joan told her.

For answer Felicia led her to the stairs.

"Now help me check these boards."

She started at the top of the stairs and Joan at the bottom examining each step with care. It was several minutes later before Felicia looked up.

"Find anything, Joan?"

"How would I know? I don't even know what I'm looking for."

Felicia moved down to a step near the middle of the stairs.

"Hmm," she muttered. "That's strange."

Joan turned and looked up quizzically.

"This board is nailed to the riser," Felicia went on, "but none of the others were."

She took hold of the board with both hands and tried to raise it.

"Why are you doing that?" Joan wanted to know.

"Is there something down there to hammer with?"

Her pal looked about quickly and slipped out of her boot.

"Here, try this."

Using the heel as a hammer, Felicia set to work.

"What the termites haven't done to this poor old building, you're going to do," Joan remarked.

"Look!" Felicia exclaimed. "The board's coming up!"

"Isn't that what you expected with all that hammering?"

Rosetta turned quickly back from the window.

"Here they come!"

"They're leaving the mine," Sherry added breathlessly, "and they're coming this way!"

"Get down!"

The girls at the window dropped to the floor and lay there tensely. There was no time to run back to the cellar. No time to do anything but lie there and pray.

Joan grasped Felicia's arm with trembling fingers and squeezed it tightly.

Motionless, they stared at one another, counting the seconds. Then they heard the welcome sound of horses' hoofs pounding down the main street of the ghost town toward the trail.

"Thank God," Sherry breathed thankfully.

When the sound of the horses' hoofs died away, Felicia turned once more to the step she had been working on.

As the step came up, she stood motionless, staring.

"Just as I thought!" she exclaimed.

Joan peered over her shoulder.

"The missing books?" She spoke incredulously, with something akin to awe in her voice.

"What else could they be?"

Rosetta and Sherry ran up the stairs as far as they could and stared in silence.

Someone had made a tin-lined compartment beneath the step just large enough to hold three dusty, dog-eared old journals.

Felicia's fingers were trembling so she could scarcely remove the books from their hiding place.

"It's them!" she cried joyfully. "It's the county records we've been looking for!"

She carried them down to the lobby and opened the top one.

"Whatever made you think the books would be in the stairs?" Joan asked.

"I'd been thinking about the hotel," Felicia said, "and I realized that it would be one business that would be hurt a great deal by losing the county seat. Back in those days, everyone who lived any distance from Calumet City would have had to stay overnight at the hotel whenever they came to transact business at the courthouse."

"But what does that have to do with it?" Joan demanded.

"The hotel keeper would be bitterly opposed to moving the courthouse, that's all," Felicia answered. "Then I remembered that we had found one of the books under the desk. That showed that the hotel keeper had had at least one of the books."

She took a deep breath and expelled it slowly, glancing down at the book before her.

"And when Norris Jennings broke through that step," she continued, "it just occurred to me that the hotel keeper might have hidden the books in a compartment under the stairs."

"That must have been exactly what happened!" Rosetta exclaimed.

Sherry moved to the window and back to the desk once more.

"Don't you think we ought to go back to the Lazy Bar Y?" Rosetta asked, glancing over her shoulder. "Those two guys might come back, and if they do, it will be too bad for us."

"Wait a second," Joan said, her voice suddenly growing weak. "I think–"

She straightened.

"Here it is!" she cried. "We've found it!"

"Are you sure?"

"Look for yourself! There are the water rights for the stream awarded to Jacob Chandler and his assigns! That's it!"

Felicia wearily ran a hand across her grimy forehead. Somehow, she felt as though she were going to cry.

CHAPTER 14

UNTO OTHERS

I didn't think we'd find it," Sherry murmured. "I didn't think we'd find it."

"We'd better get out of here!" Joan exclaimed. "Those guys could come back. And if they do, it'll be too bad."

They got their mounts and rode back to the Lazy Bar Y as fast as possible, the precious ledger books cradled in their arms. Aunt Abigail came out to meet them.

She stood facing them, hands on her hips.

"Now where have you been?" she demanded, surveying their grimy clothes and faces. "And whatever have you been doing?"

A smile broke across Felicia's face.

"We got them, Aunt Abigail!" she announced. "We found the old records."

Aunt Abigail stared momentarily in disbelief. Then her eyes filled, and her lips began to tremble.

"You–you aren't joking, are you?" she asked. There was desperation in her voice.

"Of course not!" Joan broke in. "And you'll never guess where we found them."

Aunt Abigail called to one of the hands to take their horses.

"And you girls come in the house with me," she gasped. "I want to see that for myself!"

Felicia opened the big book and spread it on the table.

"There it is," she said triumphantly. "You can see for yourself."

Aunt Abigail studied the entry carefully.

"Praise God!" she whispered.

"Now," Sherry said, "you'll be able to keep your cattle and the ranch. You won't have to sell!"

"Did we tell you that we found out why the Jennings brothers were trying to force you to sell them the Lazy Bar Y?" Rosetta asked. "It's because they discovered gold in that mine up at Calumet City and they planned on getting it."

"Gold?" Aunt Abigail laughed.

"That's right," Joan put in "We heard them talking. They said they had taken out samples and had them assayed. They didn't actually want the Lazy Bar Y. All they really wanted was that gold mine."

"But they were afraid you wouldn't sell just that part of the ranch, so they tried to get it all," Joan added.

Aunt Abigail wiped the tears from her eyes.

"My dears, there hasn't been any gold in that mine for fifty years or more," she said at last. "It's been worked out."

"But they discovered it again," Felicia told her.

Aunt Abigail shook her head.

"What they discovered was part of one of the biggest hoaxes ever tried in Colorado," she went on. "A pair of crooks got hold of the Calumet City mine and tried to sell it to a group of wealthy Easterners who came out to buy up gold-mining property. They did what we used to call 'salting' the mine. They loaded shotgun shells with gold dust instead of lead shot and fired them into the rock."

She started to laugh again.

"They made the most beautiful gold vein anyone ever saw, but the Easterners weren't as green as they looked. They got onto the trick, and both crooks were caught and served long jail sentences. If Norris and Will Jennings had asked any old-timer, they could have found out that the mine was worthless."

When they stopped laughing, Rosetta spoke firmly.

"And the first thing in the morning, I'm going along to help tear down the dam and send the water back on your side of that fence." Her face looked angry as she spoke, and her voice took on new venom. "I'll enjoy watching the Jennings' herd stand over there without getting any water! Maybe they'll find out what it's like!"

"Oh, no!" Aunt Abigail exclaimed quickly. "I couldn't do that."

Rosetta stared at her.

"Why not? That's what they did to you. It'll serve them right."

"But that's not the Christian way," the ranch woman answered. "There always has been water enough in the stream for both ranches. I can't be selfish enough to keep the Block 8 cattle from getting what they need."

Amazement filled Rosetta's eyes.

Later, the girls went to the dining room for dinner. Felicia and Joan were talking and laughing excitedly, and Sherry joined in. But Rosetta was quiet and very much preoccupied.

"What's the matter," Joan asked, "don't you feel well?"

Rosetta picked up a fork absent-mindedly.

"I feel all right, I guess."

Felicia noted the concern in her voice.

"Is there something troubling you, Rosetta?" She spoke gently.

"I haven't been able to get Aunt Abigail out of my mind, that's all."

"What do you mean?"

Rosetta swallowed with difficulty.

"I've been thinking about what she's going to do

tomorrow about the water," Rosetta went on. "All the time you girls have been talking to me and to Sherry about Christian things, I've been telling myself that I was just as good as any Christian."

Her voice choked, and she could not go on.

"But this–this afternoon, I found out that I'm not. As much as I love animals and hate to see them suffer, if that water was mine, I would have kept every drop of it away from the Block 8 herd just to get even with Norris and Will Jennings."

"That's the natural way to do, I guess," Felicia answered, "but the Bible tells us that we should *love* our enemies."

"I can tell you this," Joan added. "It is Christ in Aunt Abigail who causes her to be that way. It's nothing in herself."

Rosetta nodded understandingly.

"And I want that for my life," she confessed. "I don't want to go on in sin."

Sherry's face was radiant.

"Oh, Rosetta," she exclaimed softly, "I'm so happy for you! We've been praying and praying."

* * *

The following morning Felicia and Joan were still in their cabin when Rosetta and Sherry came bursting in.

"Guess what!" Rosetta exclaimed happily. "Dad has just decided to have the top company salesmen come here for their free vacations, and he and I are going to stay on to help entertain them."

"And I'm asking my parents to let me stay on too," Sherry added.

"That is good news."

Sherry and Rosetta both glanced at Joan and laughed.

"Actually," Sherry continued, "staying on is just an excuse. We are really sticking around to watch you ride that Brahma bull, Joan."

"I might fool you," Joan said slowly. Then, realizing what she had said, she continued quickly, "And then again, I might not."

THE
FELICIA CARTRIGHT SERIES

Felicia Cartright, a petite blonde who is one of the most popular students at Wellington School for Girls, has a surprising inclination toward mysteries. If a mysterious situation arises, it either makes its way to Felicia, or Felicia somehow finds it. Though this is a bit trying for her happy-go-lucky roommate, Joan Bailey, it does prevent life from becoming monotonous. It also enables Bernard Palmer, the popular author of the "Danny Orlis" books, to write an entertaining series of stories for girls aged twelve to eighteen.

The mysteries range from a valuable missing antique to an attempt by claim jumpers to steal a deposit of tungsten ore. There's excitement and action galore—but there's also spiritual guidance and blessing because Felicia and her partner-in-adventure love the Lord and take Him into account in all their experiences.